Stuff That
Really
Matters

Joyce—

Thank you for your encouragement over the years. Knowing you has been one of life's great joys!

Blessings to you & yours—

August '98

Stuff That
Really
Matters

Establishing Priorities
For Your Business
And Your Life

(This is stuff you really should "sweat,"
because it's not <u>all</u> "small stuff.")

by
Andy Hickman, CSP

Stuff That **Really** Matters

by

Andy Hickman, CSP

Meaningful Life Publications

Copyright©MCMXCVIII

Published in Dallas, Texas, U.S.A.

Cover design and text layout by Ad Graphics, Tulsa, OK

Library of Congress Catalog Card Number:
98-91475

ISBN: 0-9664437-0-5

CONTENTS

DEDICATION

This book is lovingly dedicated to my parents, Bob and Mary Joe Hickman. Their patience with me in my youth, and support as an adult have served as an anchor in some very rough waters. At all times, I've known that their support for me was complete, their devotion unwavering, and their love absolute.

So, it is with great joy, deep respect, and abiding love that I present you with this gift.

Thanks for always being there for me.

Love always,

Bonzo

PS Hey, Wendy, I put some funny things in here for you as well!

INTRODUCTION

"Stuff..." what a cool and all-encompassing word it is. We use it every day about nearly every thing. There's "your stuff," "my stuff," "our stuff," "the kids' stuff." Even the family dog and cat have their own "stuff." Comedian George Carlin said in one of his famous monologues that, "A house is basically just a big box to put your stuff in. And when you fill it up, you just go get a bigger box!" Presently, in addition to three homes, I also have three 10' x 20' rented storage rooms for my "excess stuff!" Yes, it sure does seem that we spend a lot of time, energy, and cash in pursuit of the "right stuff."

There are all kinds of "stuff," and yet, most of it doesn't really seem to matter. This book is about the stuff that does. Of course, we all seem to take our stuff quite personally. Most of us don't want anyone else messin' with our stuff. In fact, you might be offended by some of my observations. However, if I do offend you, I offer no apologies for it. This book is not about making you feel comfortable with your stuff. Rather, it's designed to help you focus on the stuff that *really* matters.

A LIFE OF INFLUENCE

♦ ♦ ♦

George Bailey was a man who had a very wonderful life. The classic Christmas movie, It's a Wonderful Life, tells the story of an ordinary man that had extraordinary influence on the lives of an entire community. Although he did not at first consider his contribution to the world to be anything of great and lasting value, he soon found out how his influence was the most valuable thing in Bedford Falls.

Each time I watch the movie, I wonder what kind of influence I am having in my corner of the world. Do I make sacrifices and honor my commitments like George Bailey did? Do others hold me in high esteem as they did him? Although I do not desire to feed my ego with the praise of men, I do hope that my life will be significant to others. My chief concern is that I be a good role model for my children...that they can learn from my example...not just from the things I say.

1

THE TEXAS GIANT

It was another hot August day when I took my kids to visit Six Flags Over Texas. My daughters had watched the compelling TV advertisements that declared that the newest attraction was The Texas Giant: The World's Largest Wooden Roller Coaster. The TV ads showed people apparently enjoying themselves as they rode around the track at speeds in excess of 60 MPH. My precious little girls had the bug to actually ride this monster, and I knew what that meant...I would have to ride it with them! And, since they are twins, I knew that I would have to ride it twice! Before going to the amusement park that day, I was sure that I would come up with something to say that would dissuade them from riding it. You know how it goes: "Who was it that said this would be a 'cool' thing to do? Girls, do you think it's *really* safe? Just what does a termite look like? Does the term 'wood rot' mean anything to you?"

In spite of my best efforts to put doubt in their minds, they were determined to get on board. It was like a rite of passage for them. By riding it, they would in effect be saying that they are growing up. Actually, I don't know what I was more afraid of: the roller coaster, or their desire for independence.

Lauren was the first to attempt it. As we stood in line waiting for our turn, we could hear the screams of delight (?) from the other riders that were being hurled from side to side by the relentless beast. It was at this point that Lauren said, "Papa, I think I need to go to the bathroom." I offered to take her, and assured her that she did not have to ride it. However, she declined, stood her ground, and boarded the train. As we began the long ascent up the hill, she asked me to put my arm around her and then she asked me to pray. Naturally, I did both. I held her very tightly as I prayed for God's protection, all the while hearing the incessant clink of the chain as our train was approaching the top. It was about this time that we went over the edge...

When it was over, the look on her face was one of utter victory! Her hair was tousled and tangled, but her face glowed with the light that shines most brightly from a child's pure heart. Finding a quiet place away from the crowd, I knelt down so that I could look her in the eye. Then, I told her, "Lauren, this is a day that you will always remember. For this is the day that you rode the Texas Giant! And Lauren, throughout your life you will encounter other Texas Giants...problems that are immense in size...seemingly unconquerable. When you encounter them, remember this day, and handle all of your future problems like you did this one: First you were willing to face your fear, then you drew close to me and we prayed. The important thing to learn from this is that if we will draw close to each other...and put our trust in God...then together we can overcome anything!" She hugged me and said, "Papa, I sure do love you." With a tear of joy in my eye, I got her sister Leigh and we rode it in the same way. After riding with Leigh, I gave her the same object lesson.

As parents we can find object lessons almost daily that will have a lasting influence on our children. The important thing is to always be looking for those "teachable moments"...moments that are important to our children...moments that they will never forget. Here are some of the obvious ones: First day of school, of riding a bike, of swimming or diving, roller-blading, getting a new pet, losing a pet, acne, wearing braces, buying a new house or car, moving, the birth of a sibling, making or not making the team, recitals, final exams, vacations, etc.

Throughout our children's lives there are a multitude of teachable moments...moments when their hearts and minds are open to receiving our parental wisdom. It's our job as parents to make the most of such moments. Never let one pass you by...you'll need every one of them!

2

"OH NO!

WHAT IS SHE GOING TO DO THIS TIME?!"

This is the thought that suddenly flashed across my mind one evening while eating dinner at a restaurant with the family. We were all having an enjoyable meal until the lady at the table next to us was asked the following question by her husband, "So, Honey, how was your day today?" The foolish man. He should have never asked.

This woman began a 20 minute tirade of negativity about all that was wrong in her life at work: "My boss is a moron!...My coworkers are stupid... They keep it too cold at the office...Nobody else is doing their job...The management is too cheap... My customers are idiots...Why do I have to work in the first place?...If you had a decent job I wouldn't have to!"...on, and on, and on... In the entire time, this woman did not have *even one* pleasant thing to say. Mind you, we weren't eaves-dropping. She was speaking so loudly that we couldn't even carry on a conversation. Her voice had the tonal quality of fingernails on a chalk-board!

I watched my 11-year-old daughter Leigh very carefully through all of this. Leigh is my irrepress-ible warrior child. Her passion for championing the cause of the weak is unmatched. She looks for every opportunity to do the right thing. When she notices that the scales of justice are a bit askew, she actually does something about it. The only problem is, you never know exactly *what* she will do or say!

We were on pins and needles as we watched helplessly while the following events unfolded: First, Leigh got *that look* in her eye. (Although I wasn't there to see it, I'm sure it must have been the same look that Christ had on his face just before he threw the money changers out of the Temple! Or, the look David had when he walked up to the towering Goliath, with his slingshot and 5 smooth stones!) When Leigh gets *that look*, there is <u>no</u> stopping her! Next, she slowly rose from her chair...stepped over to the woman...extended her hand...and said, "Please excuse me. My name is Leigh Hickman, and I just wanted to tell you what a beautiful dress you have on. I couldn't help but admire how well it fits you and how perfectly the color matches with your hair. Would you mind telling me where you bought it so that I could get one like it for my mother?" The lady was clueless as to what Leigh was really trying to do. The woman, completely taken aback by this unexpected line of questioning, said, "Uh, well, thank you. Actually, this dress was a gift to me from my husband. Dear, where did you buy it?"

We all watched in utter amazement at how deftly Leigh handled this difficult woman. The woman and her husband continued to visit with Leigh for another five minutes. At the end of that time, the woman was now smiling, cheerful, and best of all...quiet! Leigh is a master at reading people's moods, and was able to turn this woman's entire disposition around by asking her a very simple question. The fact that Leigh would risk doing such a thing no longer surprises me. I just wish I knew what she was going to say before she says it!

I've certainly learned a lot from Leigh. She has taught me that boldness is a virtue to be admired, (and often reckoned with!) Her passion for doing the right thing is based on her complete trust in God to guide her in every situation. She knows no fear of rejection. She will not acknowledge fear, but rather trusts in the mighty hand of her Lord. She's certainly a delight to behold. However, I just hope she never gives me *that look!*

3

LITTLE LEAGUE AND BIG LESSONS

My son Landon has taught me that winning isn't everything, but getting a snow cone after the game just might be! When he was in T-Ball, I was your typically supportive, yet anxious, parent. Although I didn't require him to be the best player on the team, I did want him to do his best. Nearly every day, either his mom, his sisters, or I would practice with him. While he wasn't the most gifted ballplayer at 6 years of age, he was easily one of the cutest!

I'll never forget the day that he made a big hit and ran around all the bases. Upon reaching home plate, the crowd filled with parents, cheered wildly for him saying, "Way-to-go, Landon! You're The Man!" and "That's MY boy!" (Guess who said that!) All the while Landon just stood there with his feet firmly planted on home plate...basking in the glory of the cheers. Eventually he walked to the dugout to receive more praise from his teammates. But, by the last inning, his team was down by three runs and it looked like a loss was inevitable.

Being the competitive person that I am, I told Landon he had to hit another home run in order for his team to win. This is when he spoke the very wise words that put it all in perspective, "Chill out, Dad. We're still gonna' get the snow cone."

I guess he was right. Often we parents put far too much importance on winning, and far too little importance on why the kids are playing in the first place...for fun. Landon had his own reasons for playing...not mine. I've learned to respect his point of view, and in the process, I've learned that rainbow snow cones really are the best!

4

DESCRIPTIVE NAMES

One evening, while attending a bible study with my daughter, Lauren, I had an opportunity to have a lasting influence on the lives of my children. The leader of the group had asked the parents to introduce their children to the other members of the group. The parents went around in turn telling the given names of their children..."This is Bobby, Sally, Mark, etc."

When it was my turn, I told them, "Although only one of my three children is here tonight, I will tell you each of their names. But, before I do, I want you to know that I have given each of them descriptive names in addition to their given names. I did this because of Christ's example in the 'Lord's Prayer.' There Jesus said, 'Our Father which art in heaven, Hallowed be thy name...' When Jesus chose a name to describe the Father, he chose Hallowed, or Holy, because the most descriptive word that encompasses the character of God is

His *holiness*. Indeed, in every thing: His justice is holy; His righteousness is holy; His love is holy; His grace is holy; His mercy is holy...the character of the Father is best described as Holy. With this in mind, it is my pleasure to introduce to you my daughter named Wisdom. However, you may know her by the name of Lauren. Her descriptive name is Wisdom, because she consistently makes wise choices. My other daughter, Leigh, is named Passionate, because she is a passionate lover of God. My son, Landon, is named Encourage, because he is constantly looking for ways to encourage others." After saying this, my daughter Lauren (Wisdom) was beaming with appreciation for my honoring her publicly in this way.

My reason for doing this was three-fold: 1) I wanted to make it public so that others would expect her behavior to be consistently wise. 2) I wanted to raise the bar, or standard, of what I expect from her. 3) Knowing that many others would be watching her through this lens, her behavior would much more likely actually be wise.

If you are a parent, try doing this sometime. First determine what one word best describes the character of your child. Then, in private, call him/her by this name and tell them why you are doing so. At the appropriate time, introduce him/her to others by this descriptive name. Your naming of him/her in this way will serve as a subconscious reminder to your child regarding the behavior that you expect to see. And, this will create a memory for both of you that won't ever be forgotten.

5

Yo-Yos and Other Stuff

Another person that has had a large influence on my life is Bunny Martin. Bunny is a man with an unusual name and an even stranger skill. He is the "World's Yo-Yo Champion." We met one summer while I was working at a Christian conference center. I was amazed with what this man could do with a yo-yo. He could do all the "standard" tricks, and much more. Once, he carefully balanced a quarter on each of my ears. Then, while he held a yo-yo in each hand, he wedged my head between the two flying yo-yos...coming ever closer to the sides of my head until Plink! Plink!...he knocked both coins off my ears! (He asked if I was "OK", but I didn't hear him!) Next, he had me hold a match between my clinched teeth and then proceeded to light it with a yo-yo! Bunny definitely knows how to *capture* your attention! In addition to yo-yoing, he did some very impressive magic. Knowing that I'm not the most coordinated person around, instead of pursuing yo-yos, I asked him to teach me some magic. Bunny agreed to teach me, and then he did something that was very wise.

Instead of teaching me some simple little magic trick, the very first thing he taught me was extremely difficult to do. It wasn't so much of a trick, but rather a "move" with cards. He told me that when I had mastered the move, then he would teach me more. His words reminded me of the scripture that says, "To him that is faithful with a little, more will be given." - Matt 25:23.

It took me six months of daily practice in front of a mirror before I had it down pat. I made a trip to his home town and proudly showed him that I could do it. He was thrilled, (and I'm sure highly surprised!), that I had accomplished it. From that day forward, until this one, I still practice almost 2 hours per day. In retrospect, I'm thankful that he didn't teach me some simple little trick that I could easily do for my friends. I learned a lot from Bunny, but the most important thing I learned was that if I was ever going to be a master at something, then I must be willing to work at it daily.

6

THE POWER OF
A DREAM

"I have a Dream!..." When Dr. Martin Luther King, Jr. first spoke these words, his hope was that we too would share in his vision for the future. He probably did not realize just how profoundly his life and his words would stir those of like mind and heart. Dr. King knew the power of a dream, and lived his life in unrelenting pursuit of it. He saw that we needed a dream...a vision for a new reality...one that would stretch us...one that would get us out of our comfort zones. Dr. King believed that all persons, regardless of race, creed, or color, should be valued by society in this way: "...not by the color of their skin, but, by the content of their character!" His belief was that we are <u>all</u> *designed* to achieve a great and noble purpose...free from the fear and selfishness that would enslave us. I too share his belief. Do you?

You'll notice that Dr. King did not say, "I have a strategic plan!" And I'm so glad that he didn't. A strategic plan is great as long as the plan is based on a heartfelt passion for your dream. But, in order for a strategic plan to be accomplished, it must be fueled by the power of the dream. Having a strategic plan is fine as long as it is powered by the power of a well-focused dream. A strategic plan is like planning a trip to take in your car...unless it is fueled by the power of your dream...you're not going to get very far!

Sadly, we often lose sight of our dreams. Remember when you were a kid and you had so many dreams about your future. Perhaps you were going to be an astronaut, an actor, an artist, a doctor, a lawyer, raise a family, or simply have enough money to live an "easy" life. Somewhere along the way, we bought into the idea that dreams are for "dreamers." They are not sensible, and therefore should be ignored. As we have grown-up, we have also *grown-away* from the joy of, and power of, our dreams. To help me combat this, I enlisted the help of my seven year old son, Landon.

One day while driving in the car, I asked Landon what he wanted to be when he grows-up? He began by telling me that he didn't want to be limited by choosing just one thing. He wanted a whole world of experiences! As he began to list all that he wanted to do, see, experience, and become, I made some notes. I then compiled them into a short tome called, "Landon's Book of Dreams." Here is a partial list of some of his dreams.

Landon wants to:

Be a fighter pilot flying the B-2 Bomber or F-16 Falcon.

Be a professional actor making movies with Harrison Ford.

Write a screenplay for a movie dealing with the future.

Own houses in Hollywood and Hawaii.

Own a golden retriever, a cat, and several snakes.

After making a list of his dreams in a special journal, we then fully discussed each one of them. I showed him that each one of his dreams requires its own special set of skills or abilities. For example: to be a fighter pilot, he must have an excellent education, with a strong foundation in mathematics. For this he started spending more time at the computer playing math games. To write a screenplay, he must have a good command of language and be able to put his thoughts into words that others will find interesting. Here, he started writing original compositions in the word processor. He also developed a voracious appetite for reading. To be a professional actor, he would need to exercise his creativity in role playing activities. For this we practiced improvisations of him in various scenarios, because like most seven-year-olds he loved to play "pretend" games. He and his sisters would put on plays depicting scenes from *Romeo and Juliet*, *The Phantom of the Opera*, *Grease*, *Annie*, *Braveheart*, *The Princess and the Pea*, *Sleeping Beauty*, *The Lion King*, etc. One day while he was standing in the outfield, his coach and I were shocked to hear him quoting Hamlet's Soliloquy. Of course this means either he has a great propensity to recite the classics, or that he just doesn't get enough balls hit his way!

The message that I tried to emphasize to him was that if he wanted to have any or all of these experiences then he must keep his options open. I told him that the better his education...the more options he will have. Also, to take full advantage of these options, he must avoid using drugs and alcohol. He will also need to develop a network of people that can help him achieve his dreams.

If you are a parent, take a methodical approach to helping your children identify their dreams.

Instead of simply asking them, "What do you want to be when you grow up?" try asking questions like: If you could go anywhere at all, where would it be? How long would you be gone? Would anyone go with you? How would you get there? What would you need to take along? What do you want to accomplish on your journey? Where else would you like to go?

Challenge your children by asking them to identify their favorite places, people, and things. Ask them why these are their favorites. Listen carefully to their answers, because hidden within them are the keys to opening the doors to that which delights their hearts. Although the desires of their hearts may be different from yours, they are nonetheless important to your children. Remember, your job is not to clone yourself through your children...keeping them in your nest...but rather, to teach them how to fly!

Once you and your children have identified what delights their hearts, make a written list. You and your child might want to title this, The List of Dreams. The activities and things on this list will be the primary motivating factors for your children. By knowing what truly motivates your children, you will be better prepared to guide them toward those activities and things that will ultimately bring them the greatest satisfaction.

After creating the List of Dreams, then discuss each one with your children to determine how they *can* achieve them. Above all things, do not be a pessimist! Be proactive! Be creative when discussing the barriers to achieving each one of them. Just because *you* may have stumbled over one of the barriers doesn't mean that your child will. In fact, your experience can help your child identify such roadblocks and develop a strategy for turning roadblocks into stepping stones.

List what is necessary for the achievement of each one: How much education, money, time, or talent is required? Do the things in their list conflict with each other. If so, gently point this fact out to them. (A brain surgeon that freelances as an off-shore welder when between jobs as a fashion photographer...well, you get my drift.)

Perhaps you will want to discuss with them people from history that have achieved many remarkable milestones through their hard work, tenacity, faithfulness, inventiveness, creativity, and vision. People like: Alexander Graham Bell, Marie Curie, C.S. Lewis, George Washington Carver, Neil Armstrong, Fanny Crosby, William Shakespeare, Eli Whitney, Joan of Arc, Benjamin Franklin, Harriet Tubman, Thomas Edison, Jane Goodall, the Bronte' sisters (Anne, Emily, and

Charlotte), General George S. Patton, Florence Nightingale, etc.

By helping your children to focus on their dreams and then documenting a plan for realizing them, you will be doing your children a great service. You will also have a better idea than you do now about what truly motivates them, what delights their hearts, and how to help them overcome barriers to their success. In short, you will be exercising influence. I believe they call that..."Parenting."

7

PARENTAL INFLUENCE

D oes just having a car make you a professional race car driver? Does owning a violin
make you a maestro? Does owning a plane
make you a pilot? Does having a child make you a
parent? The correct answer to all of these questions
is – no.

Simply giving birth to a child, and parenting
are not one and the same. While most people can
perform the basic biological functions necessary
to have a child, not all of these same people are
effective parents. Effective parenting is learned
and requires a total commitment on the part of
the one that desires to have a positive influence
on their child.

Effective parenting requires a commitment on
the part of the parents to influence their children
by modeling God's unconditional love. Unconditional love is the type of love that God demonstrated

to us through His son, Jesus Christ. With this unmerited and unconditional love, He loved us even to the point of death. His love for us is so absolute that there is nothing that can separate us from it. We are His beloved. Just as you no doubt consider your children to be the apple of your eye, you too are the delight of God's own heart.

Many times it is difficult for me to love my children unconditionally. This difficulty arises due to the fact that unconditional love is not a normal, or naturally human, form of love. It is a supernatural love. To get a glimpse of this kind of love, I suggest that you read I Corinthians, chapter 13. There you will see that without God's perfectly unconditional love we can accomplish nothing of true and lasting value. However, if we possess and practice the fine art of unconditional love, then we will see the results of using the most powerful force in the universe.

If you are already committed to loving your children unconditionally, then you will want to accept this Parent's Pledge as your own.

On my honor as a parent I will:

- Share unconditional love, laughter, and life with my children.

- Do my best and expect the best from myself and my children.

- Develop Godly character in myself and my children based on God's vision and values.

- Be truthful and honest with my children at all times.

- Teach and lead by example.

- Encourage my children to excel in the activities that delight their hearts.

- Accept my children enthusiastically and completely as they are.

- Find and develop strengths in every one of my children.

- Treat my children with dignity and respect.

- Change yelling, telling, and commanding...to asking, listening, and leading.

- Demonstrate a clear link between expectations, performance, and outcomes.

- Model a life changing relationship with Jesus Christ.

*Signed:*_____

Date: _____

I encourage you to sign, date, and then post this Parent's Pledge on your refrigerator door... right along side the picture of a fire engine that your child drew. (At least *I think* that's what it's supposed to be!)

By making this Parent's Pledge publicly known, you will be demonstrating to your children that you are willing to be held accountable to a higher authority. And, by *honoring* this pledge you will be more than just a Father or Mother...you will be a Parent.

Section One Summary

The Texas Giant

Find magically memorable moments to drive home a life lesson that your child will always remember.

"Oh NO! What is she going to do this time?!"

Don't stifle your child's form of expression, rather encourage it...no matter how embarrassing it may be!

Little League and Big Lessons

Understand that your child participates in activities for their own reasons, not yours.

Descriptive Names

Choose a name for your child that describes their character and then use that name publicly to help establish a standard of behavior.

Yo-yos and Other Stuff

Hard work and dedication to your dreams will make them come true.

The Power of a Dream

Help your child develop a List of Dreams because these activities/things are the primary motivators for your child.

Parental Influence

Merely having a child doesn't make you a parent. Effective parenting is rooted in learning to love your child unconditionally.

TIME STUFF

♦ ♦ ♦

My young son, Landon, is a "Time Management" expert. When he is playing with one of his older twin sisters, either Leigh or Lauren, and the pace of play becomes too hectic, he yells, "Time Out!" And, dutifully, his sisters comply. Wow! Wouldn't it be great if we, as adults, could suspend time by saying these two simple words?

Unfortunately, it's not that easy anymore. As we get older, the pace of life seemingly increases at an exponential rate, and we find ourselves like a rat trapped in a cage and unable (or unwilling) to get off the treadmill. The real problem with the "rat race" is that even if you win, you're still a rat!

1

TIME – AN OVERVIEW

Time. There never seems to be enough of it. Each of us is allotted only 24 hours each day. And we spend each minute of each day doing stuff that either will, or will not, really matter.

To establish priorities for a day, a week, a month, a year, or even for your entire life, requires a clear understanding of the very nature of time itself. Time is either our great friend or our enemy. If we make wise use of our time, we consider it as time well spent. On the other hand, if we squander this precious resource, then we consider it as a waste of our time.

Each day we can make time our friend by choosing to invest that time wisely. My dad used to often tell me, "Son, there's only just so many hours of daylight each day. And if you give any of it back, you'll never get there." This was his version of, "The early bird gets the worm." Of course, since he knew I wasn't too crazy about worms, I guess he decided to change the saying.

Tick-Tock...Tick-Tock...so move the hands of time. And, with each passing second we are either moving closer to our purpose or away from it. Time stands still for no one, and yet, a fallacy exists regarding time that is common to us all. We tend to regard time as our personal birthright or private possession when in fact we can not "own" even one moment in time. Often we jealously guard any use of our time by others because we regard our time as our "own." Of course this is absurd because we can not say that we "own" it at all! It is merely a God-given gift. Therefore, it is incumbent upon each of us to seize each moment in time and use it in the wisest manner possible. In order to make a wise choice of how to use our time, let us first look at the different states of time and the nature of each state.

We all experience time sequentially. That is: Past, Present, and Future. The Past is that state of time that is most determinate in its nature. Because we know what it contains, we can document the Past and identify, with either pleasure or pain, our reflections on Past experiences. The Present is this moment in time, and its nature is dynamic because it will be, in but a moment, the Past. The Future is that moment in time yet to be realized, and therefore its nature is least determinate. All of our fears, anxieties, and concerns lie in the Future because we do not know what will happen to us. Before we cast our gaze to the Future, let us first take a fresh look at the Past.

2

STUFF FROM THE PAST

As each of us reflects on the stuff in our Past we are reminded of various accomplishments and failures. Sadly, all too often we tend to dwell on our failures rather than our accomplishments. Of course, we can learn from our past mistakes, which reminds me of another one of my dad's sayings: "Son, you don't learn from your mistakes. You learn from how you *correct* your mistakes." In my life, I've had a lot of "correcting" to do!

The real value of the Past can be measured chiefly by the effect it has had in molding us into the persons we were *designed* to be. However, many people have a lot of hang-ups because of their Past. They relive with a kind of bittersweet memory the pains of youth, marriage, divorce, business success or failure, etc., never willing to let go of this "baggage" a.k.a. "stuff" from the Past.

These people almost enjoy having their "baggage." They walk around with it like a jet-lagged weary traveler ever clutching onto it lest someone take it away from them! They will tell you about their "baggage" too, and sometimes even about the "dirty laundry" that it undoubtedly contains! The excess weight of all that baggage exacts a mighty toll upon the person that is foolish enough to keep carrying it. I fly over 100,000 miles per year as a professional speaker, and sometimes I check my bags at the ticket counter. On one such occasion, I noticed that someone had hung some mistletoe above the baggage checkpoint. So, I asked the agent, "Is that mistletoe left over from the Holidays?" He said, "No. This is where you kiss your baggage good-bye!"

Sometimes don't you wish you could kiss all your "baggage" from the Past good-bye, and never see it again? You can, because the Past is, after all, the Past! No amount of fretting or worrying about it will change it. Therefore, do not let the Past be a stumbling block in your path toward the Future. You can remove the stumbling block of the Past in this Present moment. Actually, there will be no better time to do so. All you have to do is make wise choices in this Present moment and your Future will reflect the wisdom of those choices. Resist any temptation to dwell upon those

Past experiences that resulted in failure. The key word here is dwell. Short of a lobotomy, it may be impossible to fully forget the pains of the Past. But, <u>we can</u> make a conscious choice to not *dwell* on such things.

I have some good friends that were faced with a very difficult choice, a choice that if not made wisely, would have surely resulted in their divorce. Through this trial, they both had to learn the art of forgiveness, and how to resist the temptation of dwelling on the failures of the past. Their names have been changed to assure their anonymity. Here now is their story:

Ron, a handsome young Life Insurance Agent, was on the threshold of a very promising career in sales. His wife Pam, was highly supportive of his efforts to gain the training that he needed for this very demanding and competitive career. One evening, while Ron and I were visiting over dinner, he told me a dark secret that he had been hiding for many years. He told me that on many occasions he had had affairs with other women. He wasn't bragging. In fact, he seemed distraught and tormented by the knowledge of his sin. He also said that he had told his wife about the affairs as well. When I asked him why he had told his wife, he said that he had hoped that the confession he made to her would help him to unload his burden of guilt. He said that by telling Pam of his affairs, he felt a temporary sense of relief...as though his soul had been purged...the dirty laundry that he had locked in his baggage was now out of the bag and could be cleansed. It was as if by telling her of his dark secret, he was asking her to bear some of the burden of the guilt he was carrying. Naturally, instead of gladly accepting the burden that the knowledge of his sin brought to her, she felt betrayed, angry, and hurt.

My advise to him was that while he was not wrong in telling his wife about the affairs, he was wrong in expecting her to clean his dirty laundry! It was not her job to bear the burden of his guilt, because she was not capable of giving him the absolution that he truly needed. I told him that the proper person to confess his sin to was Jesus Christ, because Jesus paid the price for his sin, (and mine), at Calvary. Only by receiving God's free gift of forgiveness would he ever be free from the condemnation that resulted from his sinful choices. Because until he was willing to accept God's forgiveness, then, and only then, would the dirty laundry that he carried around like baggage from the past be washed white as snow. Feeling very remorseful for the pain that he had caused and recognizing that without Christ he was destined to a miserable future, Ron made a wise choice. He chose to repent of his sin, accept Christ as his Lord and Savior, and then he received total forgiveness for all of his sins.

After having accepted God's free gift of forgiveness, Ron now had to ask his wife to forgive him as well. Ron chose to humble himself before Pam and acknowledge that he had selfishly caused her to endure tremendous pain. Through much prayer and counseling, Pam chose to forgive him. Now, he had to forgive himself for all the pain that he had caused himself and his wife.

Thus began their sometimes difficult task of not dwelling on these past failures. In time, both Ron and Pam learned how to take every thought captive, so that as their memory of these events was brought to the front of their minds, they made a conscious choice to not dwell on the past. They realized that since each of them had been forgiven by God, that they must continue to forgive each other. They chose daily to not dwell on the past, but rather, they chose to dwell in the *present*. They acknowledged by their change of lifestyle that the forgiveness they received from Christ was sufficient for *all* of their sins and that there is now *no condemnation* for those who are in Christ Jesus!

I'm happy to report that the wise choices that Ron and Pam have continued to make has resulted in their now having four wonderful children, a happy marriage, and successful careers. This could not have been possible had they chosen to dwell in the past through resentment, bitterness, or an unforgiving spirit. They learned that forgiveness is the glue that bonds the brokenhearted.

So, how do we get on with our life after experiencing a disappointing past? The answer is found in forgiveness. That is, when we remember the painful experience, we can choose to not replay the tape in our minds. Our minds are filled with tapes from our Past, and like a good editor it is our job to edit out the bad scenes. This can best be done by choosing to forgive those people that have wronged us, or perhaps even forgiving ourselves. We really must choose to forgive because we too have been forgiven..."Jesus died for us while we were yet sinners." In the same way that God has forgiven us, so must we forgive. And how did He forgive us?...completely. When it comes to forgiving others, or ourselves, there are two excellent reasons for doing so: Forgiveness replaces bitterness, and it's the right thing to do!

Conversely, to dwell on past failures, is to postpone your growth and delay your journey to a beautiful Future. You may be thinking, "Me? A beautiful Future? Sounds like an oxymoron!" I say yes, YOU! For you were *designed* to experience an abundant life, one bursting with unimaginable opportunities! Continue reading the next chapter and discover that the magic of the Future is in YOU!

CREATING YOUR FUTURE

O f the three states of time, Past, Present, and Future, it's the Future that holds the most mystery. One of my favorite stories is, "The Lady or the Tiger." Here, a man is given a choice between two doors. Behind one is the lady of his dreams, and behind the other waits a tiger that will surely devour him. The poor fellow is sweating bullets not knowing which door will open up to a favorable future.

Many times, don't we feel like that poor guy? When faced with even a limited number of choices, oftentimes we feel paralyzed with the fear that we will make the wrong choice. It is this fear of the future that causes us to regard the future as something beyond which we can control. My hope is that in this chapter you will lose your fear of the future by discovering the key that will unlock its door and make the future not seem so mysterious after all.

Each of us has the power to create the kind of future that we want to have. All the "magic" that we need to create the future resides inside of each one of us. I believe that. But, apparently a lot of other people don't. Evidently a host of people do not believe that they have the power to control their destiny. I say "evidently," because these same people are the ones that call those 1-900-Psychic numbers. This "Psychic Business" is flourishing. You've heard of them in Newspaper, TV, Radio, even on the Internet. Just think, now all you have to do is call up a total stranger...pay them $4.00/ min...and all of your questions about the future will be solved...BOGUS! Heck, if I could tell you with unerring accuracy what the future holds for you, I certainly wouldn't be running any ads...I'd own Wall Street!...I could put Vegas out of business in about 48 hours! But, I did get curious once and called one of those numbers. The first thing the guy wanted to know was what my credit card number was. I said, "Hey, pal! You tell me!" Needless to say, it was a very brief conversation.

These "Psychic" businesses prey on the naiveté of those who would trust their Future to someone other than the person responsible...themselves! There is something appealing, almost "magical," about trusting someone else with our future. However, as a trained magician myself, I assure you that trusting others with your future is merely an illusion. The reality is that the responsible party in determining your future is not someone else, it is you! And rightly so.

But, hey, if you want someone to reveal the secret that will unlock the door to your future, I'll do it for you. I'm about to reveal to you the magical key that will unlock the mystery of your future. By using this key, you can determine precisely what the future will look like. I don't need tarot cards or a crystal ball either. Are you ready? Good. Here goes. Your future, (and mine), will be determined by only two things:

> The *choices* that we make, and the *commitments* that we honor.

It is, at once, as simple and as profound as that. There really isn't any magic formula or talisman that can determine our future. However our future will be, and should be, determined by each of us as we take <u>Personal Responsibility</u> for it!

We always have a choice in determining our future. Even the effect of circumstances beyond our control can be harnessed by how we choose to respond to them. Regardless if the door you open has a lady or a tiger behind it, it will be your choice to either embrace the one or tame the other. Each of us has arrived at this point in time due to choices we have made and commitments we have honored. Therefore, let us look at what we can do in this present moment to create the Future we desire.

4

THE PRESENT

All this talk about the Future brings us to the Present, because the Present, unlike the Past or the Future, matters the most. For this Present moment is that portion of time that most clearly resembles eternity itself – because it is in this Present moment that we make choices and honor, or dishonor, commitments that will determine our Future...our destiny. This Present moment, unlike the Past or the Future, is that moment in time where we create our Future. Or to put it another way, this Present moment is simply the raw material from which we manufacture our Future. Therefore, if we are to create an agreeable Future, then we must make wise choices and honor our commitments in the Present!

Perhaps you are haunted by mistakes from the Past and are therefore fearful of the Future. Please don't despair, for you and I were given this day as a gift from God. This day, like no other, contains all the "magic" that you need. For this day was created by God and given to you as a Royal Gift. It is brimming with hope and promise! And although I may not know what the Future holds, I know who holds the Future! All you have to do is resist the temptation to dwell on Past failures, make wise choices and honor your commitments in the Present, and then you will be forecasting your own Future!

5

THE BONSAI PRINCIPLE

I n order to seize this Present moment, and all the days in our Future, we need to consider the lessons that can be learned from a small Bonsai tree.

Ever since watching the movie titled, <u>The Karate Kid</u>, I've been fascinated with Bonsai trees. One of the principle characters in that movie, Mr. Miagi, is a wise old man that tutors a young boy named Daniel in the art of Karate. Although Daniel wanted to take a fast-track to learning how to fight, Mr. Miagi chose to teach him karate by using some very unorthodox methods like: waxing the floor, painting the fence, and polishing the car. Daniel grew very tired and frustrated with Mr. Miagi, because Daniel did not recognize that he was actually learning the art of Karate while performing each of these tasks. Eventually, Daniel goes into Mr. Miagi's workshop and notices the old man pruning a small Bonsai tree. Daniel watched with great interest as the old man carefully snipped away at the tree while forming it into a thing of true beauty. Mr. Miagi told Daniel that if he wanted to have a beautiful life, then he must treat all of life with such care.

Shortly after watching this movie, I went to a nursery and bought a Bonsai tree. The one I picked out was stunningly beautiful and stood a mere six inches in height. The nursery owner told me that the tree that I had purchased was 30 years old, and it should be 40 feet tall. I looked at him rather puzzled as I did the math…"Let's see…it's 30 years old…it should be 40 feet tall…but, it's only six inches…hum, must be no Miracle Grow!" The nursery owner answered, "No. The Bonsai tree that you are holding was never designed to be small. In fact, it was designed to be very tall. But, since it was planted in a little pot, it will only achieve a small portion of its potential."

This got me to thinking. Isn't it the same way with each of us? We weren't designed to achieve only limited success. We were designed to achieve a great and noble purpose. Then, how come we don't achieve all that we were designed to achieve? Could it be that it's because each of us has a pot around us that is holding us back and limiting our potential? And if it is, who built the pot?

Many times we build the pot ourselves. It's made with the following ingredients: Doubt, Guilt, and Excuses. Here's the recipe:

Take some doubt in your ability, mix it with a large measure of guilt from your past, and then pour on a lot of excuses.

Form it into a shape that will limit your thinking, and then put all of it into the kiln of life.

Now, simply let it bake for a lifetime.

When ready, take it out of the oven.

Hide it in the mantle of your heart.

And then you will have a convenient icon that you can point to on that day when you are asked by your Maker *why* you didn't do more with your life.

This is a tragedy. Because we were not designed to live like a little Bonsai tree! However, many times we ourselves build a pot of self-doubt around us. Our pot can be formed through thoughts like: "Sure, I could be more successful, but maybe I'm not smart enough...or young enough...or old enough...or rich enough...or thin enough." Or, we blame our lack on others: "The reason I'm a failure is because my parents are alcoholics, and that makes me codependent... so I can't do anything." Or, we fail to embrace change at work because: "I've been doing the same thing, the same way, for so long...I'm not sure if I *can* change." (What this person usually means is that they are not sure if they *want* to change.) Or, we are held hostage by our past: "I did some stupid things in the past and I can't seem to forgive myself for doing them."

All of these thoughts help to form a pot around us that will limit our potential. However, the good news is that these thoughts are merely an illusion. The reality is that we were designed to achieve greatness, and *we can* if we will only break the pot! By breaking the pot, we release ourselves to become all that we were designed to be...a person of great stature...living a noble life...achieving all that God put us here to accomplish. We break the pot by taking these negative thoughts captive the moment that they enter our minds.

Then, we reject them for the lies that they are, in favor of what God's word says is true about each of us. And that truth is that we are the beloved of God.

The world may try to tell us that we are no good, that we will be failures, and that we are not deserving of love. That, my friend, is a lie. Once again, the truth is that each of us are indeed the *very beloved* of God!

If there is one overriding theme to the scriptures, it is that God's love for us is unconditionally absolute and He is passionately pursuing a relationship with us. His greatest desire is for us to live our lives with purpose and meaning. He wants us to *know* him – not simply read about him or merely acknowledge that he exists. Because, only by truly knowing Him can we ever fully know ourselves and realize our potential. That which He has loved He has saved, and that which He has saved He will sustain. His love is liberation, and He came to liberate the captives.

Do you fear that you are trapped in a pot of worry and self-doubt...seemingly unable to take control of your life and your future? These fears are but an illusion. God wants to see you break the pot because He didn't design you to live in it! Rather, you were designed and created to accomplish all that God has planned for you. So, if you have a self-imposed pot around you that is holding you back, just go ahead and break it!

After breaking the pot, plant the roots of your life in the rich and fertile soil of God's unconditional love. There, you will flourish, blossom, and grow into the beautifully purposeful creation that God designed you to be.

Section Two Summary

Time is experienced sequentially. That is: Past, Present, and Future. The unique nature of each tense of time presents important choices for each of us to make.

Past

The Past has a determinate nature. It can be documented and remembered, but not changed. While we may not be able to forget the pains of the past, we can choose to not *dwell* on them. We can check our "baggage" from the Past at the counter of forgiveness. Forgiveness is the glue that bonds the brokenhearted.

Present

Of the 3 tenses of time, the Present matters the most. The present is the moment in time when we create our future. It is a Royal Gift from God – brimming with hope and promise!

Future

The Future, by its very nature, is least determinate. All of our fears, anxieties, and worries lie in the future. We must take <u>Personal</u> <u>Responsibility</u> for our future, because our future will be determined by only two things:

> *the Choices that we make and the*
> *Commitments that we honor.*

The Bonsai Principle

Like the Bonsai tree, we were not designed to be small in our achievements. We can seize this Present moment...break out of the mold...and create a magical Future.

LEGACY STUFF

♦ ♦ ♦

This may sound shocking, but no human being will ever read this book. (No. That's not what my publisher said!) The simple fact is that neither you the reader nor me the writer are human *beings* at all. Rather, we are human *becomings*, and we have the power to choose what that will be. We are like travelers on a grand journey. Although there are many places we may choose to go, and wondrous worlds to explore, our final destiny will be determined by how well we have weathered the sometimes tumultuous journey. Since we are all becoming something, what we become will be determined by the choices we have made and the commitments we have honored. Our legacy, too, will be determined in this manner.

1

ON BEING REMEMBERED

Ultimately, we will all be remembered by others in some way, and how we are remembered will be based largely upon how we have made other people feel. Think of someone that you have known very well that has died. In your remembrance of them, what emotion do you feel when thinking of them? Is it happy, sad, grateful, proud, angry, peaceful, etc. As you see, your remembrance of them is tied to the emotion that thinking of that person evokes in you. In the same way, another person's remembrance of you will be based not so much on what you've said to them, but rather on how you have made them feel. As a speaker, I've noticed that the feeling that the audience has about me as a person oftentimes matters more to them than the cleverness of my words.

Try this. Think of someone that you know very well, and identify the emotion associated most strongly when thinking of that person. Perhaps you feel happy, sad, angry, disappointed, bitter, encouraged, elevated, etc. Just thinking of that person will illicit a strong emotional response in you. Now, how do you suppose that other person would feel if they thought of you? Would their response to your name be the same? Here's an idea. Why don't you ask them to try this little experiment with you? By asking them to do this with you, you will have demonstrated to them that you value their relationship. Of course, to have such a frank discussion may make both of you feel a bit vulnerable. However, to do so will no doubt lead to a *lively* conversation, and it will help to unsnarl the lines of communication. Understanding how you are perceived by others can even improve the legacy you leave behind.

I have come to learn one of the keys to preserving healthy relationships with friends and family is based on such frank conversations. Without it, secret bitterness between the parties can start to grow like a fungus in the bathtub...not a pretty sight! For years I often hid my true feelings from people so as not to offend them. In the process of doing so, I developed a hollowness in my spirit...a sense that I wasn't being true with my feelings and therefore the relationship was not based on complete honesty. Then one day my Mom told me to go ahead and tell people how I really felt toward them instead of hedging. And once again, Mom was right. (Although my Mom is a great lady, I don't think she would have made much of a politician!)

Speaking of politicians, and other famous people, here are some of my favorites that have left a lasting positive legacy: Abraham Lincoln, Dr. Martin Luther King, Jr., Mother Teresa, Nelson Mandela, and Winston Churchill. Just merely reading or hearing their names evokes an emotional response from us. We remember them and what they stood for to be one and the same. They dedicated their lives in pursuit of a noble mission and we are better people because of their commitment to their ideals.

The One Word Test

Let's try something fun. Say the names of the following persons, and as you say their names, do not think about what they looked like physically. Rather, focus on what their character was like: Abraham Lincoln, Dr. Martin Luther King Jr., Mother Theresa, Nelson Mandela and Winston Churchill. When you think of each one of them, what one word best describes their character? Don't come up with a sentence to describe them. Simply think of the one word that best sums up what their legacy is today.

For Abraham Lincoln it might be Honesty, Dr. Martin Luther King, Jr. – Freedom, Mother Teresa – Compassion, Nelson Mandela – Justice, Winston Churchill – Courage. In a very real sense this one word is their legacy. We can summarize their most defining characteristic in simply one word. Each of them had the courage to make wise choices and honor their commitments, and because they did, merely remembering their name can inspire us to do the same.

Perhaps you may think that your life pales in significance to these persons...that you will never be remembered for anything as noble as these. Well, I believe you can be. In fact, I believe that the only difference between people that have actually made a difference and those that did not, can be measured by the wisdom of their choices and how deeply held were their commitments.

Making a difference...many people talk of such things...saying, "I just want to make a difference." A noble purpose for sure. Yet, they may also feel inadequate to accomplish it. A person like this would be in fine company with Abraham Lincoln. Lincoln? You ask? Yes. Just read one of the most famous speeches the world has ever known, *The Gettysburg Address*. In it you'll find Lincoln saying these words, "The world will little note, nor long remember, what we say here..." Could anything be further from the truth?! There were two speakers that day, the then famous orator Edward Everett, and Abraham Lincoln. Everett spoke for two long hours...Lincoln spoke just ten sentences that lasted two minutes...and the only speaker that made a difference was Lincoln. It's amazing to me that Lincoln obviously failed to realize just how powerful his words were then, and how highly they would continue to be valued by future generations.

What then is the one word that best sums up your life and character? Go look in a mirror and ask yourself, "What is the one word that describes my character best of all?" Or, have a friend or loved one help you determine what that one word is. Once again, this is a great way to initiate a meaningful conversation. The word you come up with might be friend, encourager, intelligent, motivator, winner, inspiring, nurturer, jerk, etc. Whatever the word is, it is influencing your behaviors because it is rooted in your self-image. Is the word one which you are proud to call your own? If so, congratulations! If not, it can be changed. And, <u>now</u> is the time to make those choices and honor those commitments that will determine how you will be remembered.

2

MAKING A DIFFERENCE

Although the luminaries mentioned in the previous chapter have undoubtedly made a lasting difference in our world, can common folks like you and me really make such a difference? Perhaps the difference our lives make will not be as well known to the public, but, the difference we make to the people around us each day is what matters most of all. Because, each day represents our opportunity to make a life altering difference in the lives of many others. Here's the story of a friend of mine who has dedicated his life to making such a difference.

A Difference Maker

He has been in and out of most of the prisons in the United States. He spends a great deal of his time on "Death Row," talking to inmates like Charles Manson. He is the co-author of the "Angel Award" winning book titled, <u>DOIN' TIME</u>. Also, he often leads the chapel service for many Collegiate, NBA and NFL teams. Most days he can be found encouraging a group of students during a school assembly. Wherever he goes, he is called to show people the "Blueprint for Life."

His name is Rick Nielsen, and I'm proud to say that he is one of my dearest friends. Rick is a fellow professional speaker, and is the person most responsible for me being a professional speaker as well. Many years ago, Rick saw some talent in me. And like a good "Talent Scout" (as he sometimes refers to himself), he showed me what my giftings were and encouraged me in my natural abilities or "talents." At the time, I was doing only magic shows for corporate parties or hawking the wares of a trade show exhibitor on the exhibit floor at some convention. Rick saw in me something that I'd never noticed. He told me that I had a real gift for speaking as well as entertaining. While I knew that my conjuring skills were pretty good, I never considered that I had anything to offer an audience other than some temporary laughs and maybe a gasp of astonishment every once in a while, (if I was lucky!) Rick encouraged me to look deep inside and try to discover the *real* magic in my heart. He told me that if I had the courage to do this, then I could have a promising career as a professional speaker.

Rick's challenge caused me to implement a technique that I often encourage others to use from the platform. That is, to focus on your goals through Planned Neglect. The technique of Planned Neglect is to focus on what you want to achieve so sharply that it causes you to have to plan to neglect activities that rob you of time and veil your vision.

For me, in order to become proficient as a speaker, it required me to neglect my number one time waster...watching TV sitcoms. By planning to neglect this one time waster, I *gained* an additional 728 hours, or the equivalent of 33 Days annually that could be used to focus on my chosen profession.

In addition to the technique of "Planned Neglect," Rick taught me another very important life-altering principle: that great people are grateful. That may sound like a small thing, but it's not. Because, a great person, or a great life, is built by doing many small and seemingly inconsequential things well everyday. Rick Nielsen is a great man because he has an appreciative attitude. After each of his speaking engagements, he sends personal "Thank You!" notes to the people that have come up to him after his presentation. Although many of these people may never be in a position to hire him, and although he may never see them again, he still takes the time to write to each one of them. Not surprising, he does get a lot of mail from these same people telling him how blessed they were by his message. The goodwill that saying "Thank You!" promotes has resulted in positive word-of-mouth advertising for him. Also, Rick doesn't discriminate when saying thanks. He is just as likely to express his appreciation to the janitor, or a student, or a faculty member, as he is to the principal. Unlike a lot of people, Rick doesn't write and say "Thank You!" thinking that it will promote his career. There is no manipulation, ploy, or self-serving motive behind his disciplined approach to the fine art of gratitude. He does it simply because it is the right thing to do! He has taught me that being thankful is a function of habit. That is, we can develop a thankful attitude by *practicing* the fine art of thankfulness.

Once I started practicing *being* thankful, I found that I actually was *becoming* more thankful. In the beginning, the practice of thankfulness was not easy for me because I was so very selfish and self-centered. At that time, I had an attitude that went something like this, "Of course good things will happen for me because I'm such a great guy." Or, "Why should I do anything special for others? They know I appreciate them." Or, "Where can I find the time to thank others? I have too much to do!" Or, "Sending a 'Thank You!' note would be a good thing to do. I'll try to do it tomorrow." (<u>Tomorrow</u>, what an illusion *that* is!)

Tomorrow

They were going to be all they were designed to be...tomorrow.

None would be braver, or kinder than they... tomorrow.

A friend who was troubled and weary, they knew, would be glad for a lift and needed it too.

On him they would call...see what they could do...tomorrow.

Each morning they stacked up the letters they'd write...tomorrow.

The greatest of people they just might have been, the world would have opened it's heart to them.

But in fact, they passed on and faded from view, and all that they left when their living was through was a mountain of things they intended to do...tomorrow.

– Unknown

In the beginning, I began to look for simple ways to express thankfulness. The key thing for me was to *practice* the art of thankfulness. First it was through phone calls, then letters to past clients. I then started doing the same for friends and family. Now, I often send a letter of appreciation to my postman, an aunt or uncle, my parents, a receptionist, a secretary, a government employee, or airline ticket agent. Disciplining myself to actually do this has resulted in tremendous benefits to me and for those that I thank. I hope you will do the same. It will make your world a far better place to live! And, you will be creating a positive legacy with which you will be remembered by all of those to whom you have said, "Thank You!"

Rick also shared with me a concept that I try to embrace everyday with every encounter that I have. He told me that saying "Thank You!" was but one small piece of a much larger work. The larger work was to become a "Builder." A "Builder" is one that seizes every opportunity to build others up, instead of tear them down. It is illustrated in the following poem. Read the poem carefully, because you will surely find *yourself* in this poem.

THE BUILDER

I watched them tearing a building down,

a gang of men in a busy town.

With a "HO-HEAVE-HO!" and a lusty yell,

they swung a beam and a side wall fell.

I asked the foreman, "Are these men skilled?

The kind you'd use if you had to build?"

He kind of laughed and said, "No indeed!

Common labor is all I need.

You see, we can easily wreck in a day or two,

what it has taken builders years to do."

So, I thought to myself as I walked away,

which of these roles have I tried to play?

Am I a builder that works with care,

measuring life by the rule and square,

building my life to a well-laid plan,

doing my deeds the best I can?

Or, am I a wrecker walking the town,

content with the labor of tearing down?

– Unknown

So, which is it? Do the choices you make and the commitments you honor reflect the light that shines so very brightly when you choose to build in the life of another? Or, have your choices and commitments been selfish with little or no regard for others? If they have been, just remember that time can be your great ally, because there is still time to write your obituary. And, wouldn't it be great if you could write your own obituary? Well, you *actually are* writing it every day on the hearts and in the minds of everyone that you encounter. How you have made others feel and whether or not you have chosen to build in their lives will be the basis for your legacy. Making the wise choice to be a "Builder" will dictate the direction of every area of your life. It will also make your life worth living.

If you would like to find out how you can live your life with a sense of purpose and meaning that will create the kind of legacy which you will be proud to leave, then read the next section and discover the Hero that lives in you!

SECTION THREE SUMMARY

On Being Remembered

We are human *becomings*, and we have the power to choose what we will become. How we are remembered by others will be based largely on how we have made them feel. We can select the one word that best sums up our character, and it will be the label of our legacy.

Making a Difference

Develop the art of thankfulness, because great people are grateful. Get in the daily habit of writing and saying "Thank You!" in creative ways.

Organize your activities by implementing Planned Neglect. That is, Plan to Neglect those activities that distract you from your highest purpose.

Become a "Builder" – One who builds in other people's lives.

Remember, you are writing your own obituary every day, in the hearts and in the minds of everyone that you encounter.

Section Four

STUFF TRUE HEROES ARE MADE OF

♦ ♦ ♦

Superman, Batman, Wonderwoman, and Luke Skywalker are fictitious characters that embody those strengths of character that we can admire. As a child, one of my favorite things was watching Saturday morning cartoons. My favorite was Mighty Mouse, because even though he was small, he could totally clobber any fat-cat that tried to tyrannically rule the lives of his tiny rodent friends. (Could this have been meant to be a metaphor for the IRS vs. us little folks?!)

Each week these fictitious characters had to overcome their fear and courageously champion the cause of the persecuted. And while it may make for entertaining TV, aren't there some better examples of true real-life heroes around us every day? And, wouldn't you like to be one of them? Well, if that's your heart's desire, then consider what Dorothy suggested in the *Wizard of Oz*, "If I ever again go looking for my heart's desire, I'll never look further than my own backyard."

1

Unsung Heroes

We are surrounded by heroes everyday. These heroes may not be wearing a cape, or tights, or have a big "S" on their chest. Rather, they will probably be wearing the disguise of a uniform: Police Officer, Fire Fighter, EMT, Nurse, Doctor, Teacher, Postal Worker, Military Personnel, Baker, Clergy, or maybe just regular clothes like you and I wear. And while they may not get the credit that they deserve, the difference they make in our communities often matters more to us than being able to leap tall buildings at a single bound. (Although, I'd really like to see that done just once!)

These kind of folks are what we admiringly call "Unsung Heroes."

A Tribute to the Unsung Heroes

"Let it never be forgotten that glamour is not greatness, applause is not fame, prominence is not eminence, stones may sparkle but that doesn't make them diamonds, the man of the hour is not

apt to be the man of the ages, a man may have money but that alone doesn't make him a success. It is what the 'unimportant people' do that really counts and determines the course of history. Even in nature, summer showers are far more effective than hurricanes, but they get no publicity. In fact, the world would soon die but for the fidelity, loyalty, dedication, and consecration of those whose names remain unhonored and unsung."

– Dr. Joseph R. Sizoo

Perhaps you too are one of these "Unsung Heroes." If you are, you probably never even considered yourself as being a "Hero" of any kind... sung...or unsung. Even though I can't see you as you read this page, I believe that you have within you the "Stuff" that true heroes are made of. That all important "Stuff" is the faith to believe that you were born to fulfill a noble mission with your life, and by fulfilling that mission, you will leave a lasting and glorious legacy!

It amazes me to encounter people that live quiet lives of desperation, never realizing or even believing that their life can make a significant difference to others. It is to these people that I say, *awaken* the Hero in you! How? You may be asking? Well, it starts with a clear understanding of why you were born in the first place.

We were all born to make a difference. At birth, we had within each of us all the potential we would need to fulfill our purpose. Although that sense of purpose that once whispered quietly in our ears may now be deafened by the shouts of an ever-demanding world, *we can* clearly hear once again the still small voice that calls us to live our lives with the courage and clarity of minstrel warrior poets.

It was my mother that instilled in me the belief that I was special, and that my life was like no other. My earliest memories are of her beautiful, smiling face and loving embrace. And with her love, she encouraged me to embrace the idea that I could accomplish all that God had intended for me.

However, there were other less encouraging voices. I had an uncle that once told me to relax in my school work. He said, "Don't work so hard...relax, because a hundred years from now, who's gonna' know the difference?" My uncle's homespun philosophy grated at my sense of purpose like fingernails dragging down a chalkboard! Because, my answer, and my mother's as well, was that maybe what we do today *really does* matter. What if a hundred years from now, I will want to have "made a difference?!" If I am to make a difference...100 years from now...or next Tuesday...then now is the time to do it!

I know that you can make a lasting difference, and it starts with how you view yourself. The scripture says that, "You are fearfully and wonderfully made." - Ps. 139:14. And, you were created to fulfill a noble mission...a mission no less noble than that of Abraham Lincoln or Dr. Martin Luther King, Jr. Both of these men were servants in the truest sense of the word. They laid down their lives so that we could inherit a better and more just world.

Although our society has embraced the idea that those who are served are to be held in higher esteem than those who serve, history and scripture tell of another story..."He among you that would be great, let him become a servant to all." Perhaps the way to achieve our purpose and become a Hero for others is rooted in serving others rather than in seeking to be served.

The greatest "CEO" of all time once held a meeting of his board. The board was highly supportive and dedicated to their leader. In fact, they wanted to be just like him. At the meeting, the board members asked, "You are a great leader and we want to be great just like you. How can we be great?" Their leader responded, "If you want to be great, even the greatest, then become a servant to all." - Matt 20:26-28.

That's kind of a tough choice, isn't it?...to choose to serve others, rather than seeking to be served. It's natural for each of us to seek our own pleasure and to merely give lip service to serving others. Rarely do we encounter a person that will sacrifice their own good for the good of another. But, that's what real heroes do, don't they? Here is the story of one who did.

His name is Jim Elliot. Jim was a successful businessman and minister that had a great deal of compassion for the less fortunate. His compassion led him to the jungles of South America and the banks of the Amazon river. Jim wanted to share all that he knew with a particular race of people – the Ankah Indians. The Ankah Indians were a primitive people that had not been exposed to the scriptures, and Jim wanted to take the message of God's love and forgiveness to them. In order to do this, Jim had to leave the comforts and safety of his home in the United States. Jim also knew that the journey would not be without great personal risk. The Ankah Indians had a reputation for being less than cordial to visitors. In fact, the very people that he went to serve, the people that he chose to risk his life for, the Ankah Indians, ended up killing Jim Elliot. Was his life wasted or his purpose unfulfilled? I don't think so.

Before he left, Jim was asked by a friend why he would leave the relative comfort and security of his home in order to serve a people that lived half a world away. Jim Elliot's answer to this question is staggering. He said, "He is no fool that will give up what he cannot keep in order to gain that which he can never lose." Wow! What a remarkable statement that is! But, what is it that we cannot keep? Ultimately, will we be able to keep our possessions, houses, cars, Country Club memberships, etc.? No. Then what is it that we can never lose? We can never lose the legacy we leave behind.

Jim Elliot realized that his condition as a human was "terminal." So it is for all of us. Since you're reading this book, I may as well tell you...none of us are going to make it out of this thing alive. The stuff that really matters to us *will* determine how we are remembered.

The choice is ours to make daily. We can either choose to selfishly cling in the present moment to things that are temporal and will one day pass away, or we can choose to peer through the lens of the future committing ourselves today to embrace a higher and more noble purpose.

2

STUFF TRUE HEROES SAY

The first step on the pathway to leaving a lasting positive legacy is to develop the habit of using the language that true heroes use. The words that proceed from our mouths can either encourage (give courage to) or discourage (take courage away) everyone around us. Indeed, the hardest thing to bridle is not a wild stallion, but a tongue.

We truly can be heroes for others. And here's some practical ways that we can:

1) Speak in such a way that each and every encounter with someone else makes that other person better off for having encountered you that day. Let all the words that proceed from your mouth be filled with healing, comfort, encouragement, and joy!

2) Even in your choice of humor make certain that you, not someone else, are the brunt of

the joke. During his Presidency, Ronald Reagan was a master at using self-deprecating humor to endear himself to the press. Who can forget what he said to his wife, Nancy Reagan, after he had been shot?..."Honey, I forgot to duck!"

As a humorist myself, I get far greater mileage with my audiences when I poke fun at me rather than them. For example: At a recent speaking engagement I experienced my most embarrassing moment. Prior to my one hour keynote which was presented in beautiful Jackson Hole, Wyoming, before a group of 200 Neonatal Nurses, I did something that all Professional Speakers know <u>not</u> to do – I drank too much water.

Thirty minutes into my speech, I started to feel the "urge"...at the end of my hour I really had to *"go!"* So, I walked out of the room...into the hall... and *ran* to the nearest bathroom! I proceeded to relieve myself, sighing heavily, and flush. After doing this, I then returned to the meeting room only to discover that all 200 nurses were pointing at me and laughing. I looked down thinking maybe my fly was open, but it wasn't. Then, suddenly I realized why they were laughing...I had forgotten to turn off my wireless microphone! They heard everything!...the zip...the tinkle-tinkle...the sigh...and of course the *flush!* I was so embar-

rassed! So, I went up to the front of the room...
thrust my fists into the air...and shouted, "I feel
like a New Man! But, I really could use a catheter
if you have one!" Fortunately for me they were
nurses so they understood.

3) Practical jokes can leave a very bad taste in
your mouth. I know, and you are about to find
out how I came to learn this. Please try to keep
in mind that I was only eight years of age at
the time that the following took place:

One evening my older brother, Wendy, our
cousin named Jay, and I were preparing for bed.
During our preparations, Wendy applied some
stuff to his fingernails that looked like fingernail
polish. Actually, it was a *very* HOT substance used
to discourage him from biting his fingernails during the night. My mother's Pekingese dog, Sophie,
was sleeping soundly in her doggy bed with her
little tongue barely hanging out of her mouth. I
don't remember which one of us three boys was
the first to come up with the idea, (surely not me!),
but we decided that it would be great fun to paint
the dog's little tongue with this nasty stuff. As my
brother brushed the hot liquid on Sophie's tongue,
the little dog instinctively brought her tongue into
her mouth. Then she developed a pained expression as she tried in vain to rid her mouth of the

foul substance. The three of us watched this and just laughed ourselves silly over it! Jay and I egged-on Wendy saying, "Do it again! Do it again!" Wendy willingly complied with our wishes. This was so much fun that we rushed to tell my mother all about it.

Upon hearing the tale, my mother asked, "So, you boys thought that was real funny, did you?" Knowing my mother's zeal for justice, it was at this time that we started to get a little worried.

The three of us boys went to bed and fell asleep. Later that night I was sharply awakened to a burning sensation on my lips. They felt like they were on fire! I licked my lips in an attempt to quench the fire, but it only made things worse because now my tongue felt like it was on fire too! My brother, Wendy, and Jay, were both experiencing the same pain. All three of us ran into the bathroom looking for water, and it was then that we saw my mother. She was standing there with a very satisfied look on her face and holding the bottle of that fingernail stuff that she had painted on our lips while we were sleeping! We each got our drinks of water as my mother said, "Oh, that was just <u>so</u> funny!" Needless to say, we all learned an important lesson that night. I'm just glad we didn't use Super-Glue!

4) Resist using (or even listening to) sarcasm, racism, sexism, cynicism and every other temptation to tear others down. These are sorry substitutes for real humor. Sarcasm, racism, sexism and cynicism have a darkness to them that is subversive in nature. These poor attempts at humor attack the character of others, and are only used by imbeciles that aren't clever enough to find, and say something, that is truly funny. They rely on "shock value" because their feeble minds haven't matured beyond the playground or locker room.

The rule of thumb is this: If there is <u>any</u> doubt as to the appropriateness of the humor you are contemplating using, *don't* use it! Ask yourself if what you are about to say will compromise your reputation, and your influence, with those in attendance. A reputation is like a shadow... sometimes it follows you...sometimes it proceeds you...but good or bad it's always with you! Is your reputation worth risking for a cheap laugh? For what price would you barter your integrity? Chances are good that your conscience is a better guide for your speech than an unbridled tongue.

5) Develop the language of a true winner. Look for opportunities at work and in your home to speak words that encourage others. Speak winning words like:

"You're a winner!"

"Terrific job!"

"I'm glad we're on the same team."

"I really admire the way you do that."

"I like who I am when I'm with you."

"You bring out the best in me."

"I'm proud to know you."

The energy which accompanies such winning language is powerful and uplifting! The real benefit of speaking such language is not limited to the hearer alone. In fact, in any conversation at least two people hear what is said...the listener and the speaker. Just by saying something like, "You're a Winner!" to someone else will automatically elevate your own energy as well! This is the secret weapon that successful teams (at work and at home) employ with enthusiasm!

Conversely the opposite is true also. Some people get in the habit of speaking the language that losers use. These sad folks I call, "Energy Suckers." And they are to be avoided at all cost! This is how they prey on others: Let's say you arrive at work feeling GREAT!...your energy is high... your attitude has been adjusted to *smokin'!*...your practically dancing down the hall...and then, you see the Energy Sucker. This pitiful soul is headed your way and there is no place to hide. You brace yourself for the inevitable barrage of negativism as they corner you saying things like: "I hate my job...I'm over-worked and _____ (Fill-in the blank. You've heard it before.)...I'm unappreciated... This is a lousy place to work...And, if all these customers would stop interrupting me maybe I could get some *work done* around here!"

After hearing all this you walk away feeling violated. Your energy has been sapped. You feel drained. The best way to get back the energy that has just been sucked out of you is to look in the mirror and speak winning words to yourself and/or connect with others that have the same winning attitude.

The next time you encounter the Energy Sucker, try telling them that they too can be a winner. When they ask you how, you can show them that there is a better way to live. And who knows, you just might plug up the hole that has been subversively draining the life out of your organization/home!

Whether it be at work or at home, we can become a Hero for others by choosing to serve rather than be served, and by taking control of our tongues. There is real power in a word lovingly spoken and a life well lived. And, as for *your* descriptive name, I say let it be "Hero"...one who chooses to build through words well spoken and a life well lived. For that is our purpose, our destiny; we were *designed* to build in other people's lives. I hope you will join me on my journey to a higher path...although the path is a narrow one...the footing is sure for those who hold His hand!

SECTION FOUR SUMMARY

True Heroes don't have to wear a cape and tights, or a special uniform...they may wear regular clothes like you or I wear. True Heroes may look common, but their character isn't.

Unsung Heroes

These have the faith to believe that they were designed to fulfill a noble mission. The path to greatness is cut with the sword of servanthood.

Language of Heroes

Let every word spoken by you be one of encouragement, healing, comfort, and joy! Use self-deprecating humor instead of put-downs. Be cautious when doing a practical joke, because the joke might be on you! Avoid sarcasm, racism, sexism, cynicism, and those that speak such things.

Speaking "Winning Words" elevates the performance of others and yourself. Resist "Energy Suckers," and don't be one yourself.

Take control of your tongue because, "The mouth speaks out of that which fills the heart." - Matt. 12:34. You can control your tongue by "taking every thought captive" - 2 Cor. 10:5, and then only speak those words that edify and encourage others. Heroes build others up because they are convinced that they were designed and destined for that purpose.

Section Five

RELATIONSHIP STUFF

♦ ♦ ♦

One of the most stunning sights on Earth is a well-kept, beautifully arrayed garden. Such a garden is filled with plants and flowers that can transform through sight, smell, and texture, the attitude of anyone that is wise enough to walk along its paths. All beautiful gardens, regardless of what species of plants grow there, have one thing in common – no weeds!

This section deals with keeping the garden of your relationship stuff free of weeds. Relationship weeds are named jealousy, anger, distrust, bitterness, and resentment. Please keep in mind, this is your garden, not someone else's. You are only responsible for keeping the weeds out of *your* garden. Let your neighbor take care of his/her own. (They probably wouldn't want your help anyway!) Otherwise, this section could go on for days.

1

TENDING YOUR RELATIONSHIP GARDEN

I f your relationships were a garden, what would it look like? Would your garden be scarcely recognizable from a veritable forest of weeds? Would it be as barren as a wind-blown desert, or would it be flourishing with well-tended plants and flowers that nourish your soul?

Since we all have, at best, limited control over other people's stuff, this chapter will be devoted to the stuff *you* can bring to having healthy relationships. While we can't control how other people respond to us, we <u>can</u> control our response to them. And, that is what we are responsible for – our response. Our response-*ability* is rooted in being able to respond to others during conflict in a healthy way. Instead of blaming others for the weeds in our relationship garden, we should simply take personal response-*ability* for our role in the relationship. By focusing our energy on cultivating our garden and doing what is right, our relationships with others will be frank, honest, and healthy. I know one couple that has done this successfully for over 50 years.

Some good friends of mine, Frank and Marge Witherspoon, recently celebrated their 50th year wedding anniversary. I had the privilege of asking them what were the secret tools that they used to keep the weeds out of their relationship and have a successful marriage. I was expecting them to say something like love, commitment, common interests, their friendship, etc. Instead, they both said that the secret tools to their success were forgiveness and gratefulness. Forgiveness and gratefulness?

Check out the wisdom in that answer! Frank and Marge are real folks, not angels. They didn't live some picture perfect type of marriage made in Heaven – free from the hassles and conflicts that we mere mortals must face. No, they experienced the same kind of stuff that every couple has to deal with. For them, the difference between success and failure was choosing to forgive the other party when they were wronged and having an attitude of gratefulness.

Just try to imagine how much better your own relationships would be if you would choose to forgive as quickly as you choose anger, bitterness, or resentment. But, anger, bitterness, and resentment do have their own pleasures don't they? We can feel almost a certain delight in harboring the pain that someone else caused us. All too often we are quick to share our pain with others with little regard for the perils of the "grapevine." Then, when the one that we are complaining about gets wind of our talk, guess what – more weeds pop up.

In order to be able to quickly forgive others we must be committed to *their* highest good as well as our own. When injured by someone else, instead of focusing on ourselves and having a pity-party, we can choose to focus on their needs and attain reconciliation by exercising both forgiveness and gratefulness unconditionally.

One of the best ways to crash a self-made pity party is to simply take inventory of your many blessings. It's kind of hard to feel sorry for yourself and continue to complain about all that you lack when you are counting your blessings. And, letting others know that you are grateful for them will certainly cultivate the soil in your Relationship Garden.

2

VALUES STUFF

Possessing an attitude of gratefulness, being considerate of another person's needs, and being quick to forgive, are a by-product of one's values. And, the word "values" has been getting a lot of press these days. Each election year, it's amusing to watch politicians claim that they are the "values" candidate. Often during political campaigns, you will hear people claim, (although heretofore you never would have guessed it!), that they are for "Family Values!" They use the word "values" as though it were some kind of pawn to be used in this elaborate game called life.

Most people when asked what they value the most will answer, "My family." But really folks, let's cut to the chase. I can tell you, the reader of this book, what you truly value the most. In order for me to tell you what you truly value the most, I don't need to look at tarot cards, a crystal ball, or even call a psychic...all I need to look at is two things: your *checkbook* and your *calendar* – because we all spend time and money on that which we value the most.

So, if you say that what you value the most is your family, but you're working 70 hours a week...playing golf on your day off...too tired from all the work to give adequate time and attention to your spouse or to play with the kids when you get home...in the space of a week you have maybe 30 minutes of meaningful dialogue with the people you claim to value the most...it simply doesn't add up. If what you claim to value is not reflected in your checkbook and calendar, then you are living an illusion. I bring this to your attention so that you can examine your own checkbook and calendar. When you do, you will clearly see what you *truly* value the most.

The results of this audit of your time and finances may or may not be pleasing. But, even if they are not, don't be too hard on yourself, because that's why you were given today – to make wise choices and honor your commitments in the present so that the legacy you leave will be reflected in your checkbook and calendar, thus revealing the values for which your life has truly stood. This day, brimming with hope and promise, is yours to use and create the legacy for which you will be remembered!

3

NURTURING DEEP ROOTS

After taking a close look at your checkbook and calendar, now may be the time to re-establish your relationships on a deeper and more meaningful level.

Here's something that can help you in any relationship, provided you are willing to regard the good of another as equal to your own. It also requires you to make certain that your checkbook and calendar are in concert with what you truly value the most. It is a covenant.

Webster's Dictionary defines a covenant to be: "1) A formal, solemn, and binding agreement. 2) A written agreement or promise under seal between two parties for the performance of some action." Sounds serious, doesn't it? Well, maybe if we are to have deeply rooted relationships with others, then we must do something radical. Although entering into a covenant relationship is not a new idea, actually *abiding by* the terms of such a covenant in today's world would certainly be viewed as radical! Just think of it as using Roundup on the weeds in your relationship garden!

I encourage you to write down this Covenant for Relationships, sign it, and then give it to those with whom you desire to have a lifelong relationship.

Honoring such a commitment to someone else will not always be easy. It will require the very best of you at all times. But hey, who ever said having a beautiful garden was easy?!

A COVENANT FOR
PERSONAL RELATIONSHIPS

Believing that these 13 promises are worthy of our relationship, I hereby enter into them with full faith and solemn agreement:

1) I covenant to give you untiring love. Nothing you can do, feel, or say will stop me from loving you.

2) I covenant to pray with you and for you. The ultimate hope for our relationship is to bring the fullness of God's grace into every circumstance.

3) I covenant to meet your needs as God gives me opportunity to do so. Your emotional, mental, spiritual, and physical needs are as important to me as my own.

4) I covenant to be honest with you. You will hear me speak the truth, measured out in love.

5) I covenant to be sensitive to you. I will relax and let your thoughts and feelings flow into me, savoring them, considering them with value.

6) I covenant to be confidential about you. You can say anything and be anything you want and I will not reject you or repeat it to anyone else.

7) I covenant to always think the best of you. I will never gossip about you or listen to the gossip of others. I will always give you the benefit of the doubt.

8) I covenant to always defend and protect you. I will build you up to other people and protect you and your interests.

9) I covenant to never judge you. I will not think less of you when you fail, and will not share your failure with others.

10) I covenant to accept you as you are. I will be patient as I watch you grow into the person you were designed to be.

11) I covenant to maintain the spirit of unity in our relationship. I will always be the initiator to make things right and to forgive you quickly with the promise to never bring problems from our past into the present.

12) I covenant to be available. I will always be willing to visit with you about anything that you deem is important.

13) I covenant to be grateful. I will practice an attitude of appreciation for you because we have been knitted together in this tapestry of life by the very hand of God.

By: _____

Date: _____

Section Five Summary

Healthy relationships have the fragrance and beauty of a well maintained garden...free of the weeds named jealousy, anger, distrust, bitterness, and resentment.

Tending Your Relationship Garden

Having an attitude of gratefulness and being quick to forgive are two vital nutrients for the health and well-being of your Relationship Garden.

Values Stuff

To determine what is most important to you, closely examine your checkbook and calendar, because we all spend time and money on that which we *truly* value the most.

Nurturing Deep Roots

Re-establish your relationships on a deeper and more meaningful level by entering into a "Covenant Relationship" with others.

BUSINESS STUFF

♦ ♦ ♦

In business, the stuff that matters most of all is developing loyal customers. We can have the best trained staff, the right product or service, the best pricing, the fastest delivery, and the latest technology, but without loyal customers we will never realize our full potential in the marketplace. Loyal customers are built on promises kept. Because nothing fuses the bond between people closer than a promise kept.

Much has been said and written about the techniques needed to build customer loyalty and excellent customer service. But, let's see what *true* "Customer Service" really looks like. Delivering true customer service is not limited to learning the skills needed to provide it, but rather, true customer service is a combination of those skills and the right attitude to go with them.

1

Is Customer Service In You?

As I speak to the leading corporations in America, one of my favorite things to do is to ask people what their job is. I get many answers like: sales, customer service, manufacturing, distribution, human resources, management, marketing, etc. Whatever they say, their answer will almost always describe their function, but rarely does their function equal their mission.

Another question that I often ask is, "Why do you get up in the morning?" To this question, I get some really strange answers. Some people will answer, "I got to." But they don't *have* to, do they? Isn't that a choice? Why, they could choose to just lie there, and if they laid there long enough even the government would send somebody by to check on them! Another answer I've gotten is, "Well, to be honest, the reason I get up is because I have to go to the bathroom." The bathroom?! Isn't that a sad commentary on our work force...millions of people standing in the bathroom every morning saying, "Well, while I'm up, I might as well go to the office."

What I'm getting at here is, *why* do you get up in the morning? What is your mission? Sadly, most people go to work and yet have no idea *why* they are there! Oh, they can tell you what their *function* is on the job, but they don't have much of a clue when it comes to *why* they perform that function. One of the dangers of having a detailed job description is that it causes employees to develop a myopic view of their role in the success of the company. These same workers will, over time, compartmentalize their thinking. Hence the oft-heard lament, "That's not my job," which kind of reminds me of one of the funniest lines said to Peter Sellers in the movie, *The Pink Panther*, when he was told, "That's not my dog."

When an employee compartmentalizes their thinking they insulate themselves in a way from taking personal responsibility for anything that is outside of their narrow job description or function. For example: if you were to ask someone in sales if they are in Customer Service they would undoubtedly answer, "No. I'm in sales." Perhaps a better question would be, "Is Customer Service *in you?*" Customer Service is not a job description, it is <u>the only</u> good reason for getting up in the morning!

Is customer service in you? Is it in your heart to meet or exceed the expectations of the customer? Are you willing to commit all that you are to satisfying the customer? All that you are, you ask? Yes! Because when you see your role in business and in life as being a Hero for others, when you choose to consider the good of another as equal to your own, when you would rather serve than be served, then and only then, will you have the kind of attitude that will assure your success in both business and in life!

Here's something that can help you do this. I wear a little button that has written on it, DIMTY. This little button represents the most compelling question that my customers, both external and internal, ask of me every day. It is an unspoken question that asks, "Do I Matter To You?" Wearing this button serves to remind me that others are asking me this all important nonverbal question. The DIMTY question, although unspoken, is always there, and I answer it most often in an unspoken way – with either interest, compassion, concern, enthusiasm, or indifference.

If I'm to build loyal customers, people that are delighted with my service, then <u>I must</u> answer the DIMTY question. I've noticed that sometimes when a customer asks me this question it is disguised as anger. They may be upset with me, but what they really want to know is, "Do I matter enough to you for you to inconvenience yourself and meet my need?" If I'm going to be their Hero then I must answer their DIMTY question with an emphatic, "YES! And so does your continued business!"

Recently, I had my DIMTY question answered while I was shopping for carpet. Mind you, I didn't want to buy any carpet for the house, but I had to because a pipe had burst flooding the downstairs area. So, with insurance check in hand I went out to visit five different stores. In the first four stores I walked in with money and I walked out with money. Why? Because evidently the store owners didn't want it. You see, I *wanted* to give them the money...I needed carpet and I needed it quick...this was not something that I even remotely enjoyed doing and I would have gladly given the money to the first person that would affirmatively answer my DIMTY question.

But, alas, my experience at the first four stores was pretty much the same. I walked in...stopped about five feet inside the door...gazed around the huge showroom...started feeling overwhelmed by the number of choices...spent about five minutes looking at some samples...and yet in all this time NOT ONE person offered to help me! Oh, yes, they were there all right...employees that evidently think that it's their job to talk on the phone, rear-range stock, discuss lunch plans, whatever! When asked by their boss, "Why are we in business?" these same employees would probably say, "To serve our customers, naturally." And yet, they all let money walk into their store...and walk right back out!

And then, I met Jimmy. Jimmy was a young fellow that knew how to answer my DIMTY question. Upon entering his store, (I say "his store" because he acted like __he__ owned it!), he stopped whatever it was that he was doing...looked me in the eye...smiled...walked over to me...welcomed me to "his" store...extended his hand...introduced himself...asked me for my name...and then asked me, "Mr. Hickman, how may I help you with a flooring need today?" I was totally blown-away!

I told him about the flooding and then he started asking me questions like, "Did you happen to bring a picture of your house with you? What style of home do you have? Is it contemporary? Traditional? Spanish? A log home? What part of the house needs new carpet? What other types of floor covering are in adjacent rooms? What color are the walls? What kind of furniture do you have?" And then he asked, "How far do you live from the store?" I told him it was about 20 minutes away. He asked, "Would you mind if we went back to your house so that I can look at it? I want to see your furniture, wall-coverings, and traffic areas so that I can make sure that the carpet you buy is precisely what you need. You see, I have many choices available and yet only one of them will be suitable for your home. In fact, the carpet you select will probably be in your home for at least 5 years...and that's longer than most marriages! Of course, there is no obligation or extra charge for this." I gladly accepted his offer.

Do you think Jimmy got my money? You betcha! And I was glad to give it to him. Why did I give it to him? Because he made it clear that I mattered to him *personally* and he was dedicated to delivering true customer service. In short, Jimmy demonstrated by his actions and attitude that he knew *why* he had a job.

Sadly, for consumers, there are far too few "Jimmys" in the workplace. But, I guess that's a good thing for the few "Jimmys" that are out there...folks out there that actually want to sell something and know how to answer the DIMTY question.

2

YOUR CUSTOMER HAS A NAME – USE IT!

I t's kind of hard to convey to (much less convince) your customers that they matter to you if you don't even know their name. Here's a subtle yet most powerful way to answer the DIMTY question that your customers are asking you...remember their name.

In the previous chapter you read that a salesperson named Jimmy made a great first impression on me. You will recall that he did several very impressive things in the very first moments of our encounter: he stopped whatever it was that he was doing, he looked me in the eye, he smiled, he walked over to me, he welcomed me to "his" store, he extended his hand, he introduced himself, he asked for my name, and then he called me by my name. There truly is no sweeter sound to your customers' ears than the sound of their own name. When you can recall a person's name they are impressed and will remember how important you have made them feel.

There is real power in being able to do this, and it's one of the best things you can do to enhance your career because it will improve how others perceive you. Have you ever considered just how others perceive you? Perhaps you've heard the expression, "Perception is reality." It's true. How others perceive you becomes reality in *their* mind. If they perceive you as being highly intelligent, it doesn't really matter if you are or you're not. They perceive you that way, so it is true as far as they are concerned. Boosting another's perception of you can be quickly, easily, and effectively done by simply improving your ability to recall names. If you are looking for a way to differentiate yourself from your competition, then learn and apply what I've written in this chapter. Then, others will perceive you as being sharp, aware, and entellijent...(OOPS! I mean intelligent!)

Before each of my Keynote Addresses, I mingle with the crowd in order to meet or overhear the names of the audience members. Then, when I call on them by name (sometimes several hundred of them) from the stage, it totally blows-'em-away! In addition to recalling their names, I ask them for their birth date and then tell them which day of the week their birthday will be on in the current year. I do this by remembering the entire calendar.

Many people in my audiences probably think that I'm brilliant, when actually, I have only an average IQ. In fact, after I took my College Entrance Exam the school counselor said that my Verbal Score was so low that I could look forward to a flourishing career as a mime! The good news is that everyone has a photographic memory. Some just don't have enough film!

After I speak, invariably members of my audience will approach me and ask, "How did you remember all those names?" And although I teach a workshop on how they can do this, I will now answer their question so that you, the reader of this book, can employ this most powerful secret weapon!

The ability to remember another person's name requires two things: Technique and (more importantly) the proper Point of Focus. Of the two things necessary, the proper Point of Focus matters the most; but first, I'll tell you about the Technique.

The technique I use is this: I connect their name to someone else that I know by the same name. For example: If the person's name is Becky, I think of someone else that I know named Becky and connect them through some similar characteristic. They may have similar hair styles, eye color, build, height, smile, tone of voice, posture, or even attitude. By connecting this unknown person to the known person, it is much easier to recall the name of this new acquaintance. If this new Becky has a hairstyle or color similar to the known Becky, then I'll picture this new Becky with her head under the faucet as the known Becky washes her hair!

Often the person's name will sound like, or remind me of, something familiar. These then become descriptive names like: Bill – dollar bill, Mary – wedding dress, Bernard – dog, Elizabeth – queen, Crystal – glass, Fred – Mr. Rogers, Michelle – my shell, Peter – apostle, Linda – lender, Rose – flower, Jack – beanstalk, Mel – melt, Beverly – hills that is, Bob – in water, Diana – princess, Joseph – colorful coat, John – toilet, Derrick – oil well, Adam – apple, Tom – cat, Matthew – tax collector, Frieda – freedom, Josh – teasing, Doug – dig, Phillip – fill up, Jane – plain, Ryan – cryin', Charlie – brown, Wade – wading, Madelyn – mad at lint, George – president, Carrie – carry, Sue – sew, Luke – skywalker, Fern – plant, Herbert – herb, Mike – microphone, Allen – wrench, David – king, Daniel

– lions, Sherry – wine, Betty – crocker, Barbara – bush, Annette – a net, Steven – stoning, Jim – gym, Harold – Hark! Angels sing, Nina – boat, Carolyn – caroling, Cathy – cartoon character, etc.

Anytime I meet someone by one of these names, I automatically think of the picture that I've previously connected to that name. This now makes their name not so abstract. It's easy to recall pictures in your mind provided that you make the pictures aCtiVE! The more action you can put with the sound of their name, the greater chance you will have in recalling their name. For example: Suppose you meet someone named George. Instead of merely picturing a portrait of George Washington, imagine that this *new* George is crossing the Delaware in the middle of the night as water splashes over the side of the tiny boat. For Michelle, you picture her walking barefooted along the shore searching for her lost seashell. She holds seashells up to her ear hoping to hear one whispering "Michelle." David is dressed in a regal robe playing his harp as he sings a song about defeating Goliath.

This really is a creative game that you can play anytime. Just think of names, form a picture, and then add action to it. You can do this! Just exercise the power of your imagination to create a memorable scene. Often the more bizarre you make the scene the easier it will be to remember it. For example: after meeting someone named Bernard, imagine him down on all fours eating out of a dog bowl as he turns and looks up at you with slobber falling out of his mouth. It may be gross and kind of weird, but you will *definitely* remember his name! Besides, he can't read your mind. Just don't ask him if he's "house-broken!"

The key thing here is to practice! The next time you're driving in your car to meet with some strangers, use this time to create vivid pictures in your mind that you can use to connect to people's names. Once you have the picture and action scene in your mind, then all you have to do is simply put the new person that you are meeting in the scene. When you get there, you can pretend that you are Steven Spielberg, and they'll never know that they have a starring role in the theater of your mind!

The second, and most important, way to remember names has to do with your Point of Focus. When you meet someone: smile, look them in the eye, shake their hand, state your name, and *listen* as they say theirs. Listening...it's more than a skill, it's an attitude of the heart.

When most people encounter someone else that is new to them, their thoughts when meeting that person are on themselves instead of on the other person. They may be thinking: Does this person like me?...Do they think I look OK?...What are they thinking of me?...etc. What these self-centered people fail to realize is that this life is not about them...it's about serving others.

To have success in both business and in life itself we must believe that the good of another is equal to our own. When meeting someone new, if we will resist the temptation to think of ourselves and focus our attention on the other person, then we have a greater chance of remembering who they are. Without this proper Point of Focus, we have <u>no</u> chance of remembering them and all our "technique" is useless.

When we have the proper Point of Focus, our objective will be in each encounter to make the other person better off for having encountered us. This requires an abandonment of ego-driven pride in oneself replaced with a passion for encouraging others. The real and lasting benefit of having the proper Point of Focus and remembering others' names is that by doing so you will find favor with others. You will develop a reputation as being one that is sincerely concerned for the success and well-being of others. These people in turn will speak well of you in your absence. They will become your "cheerleaders." In business, one can never have too many cheerleaders...people that speak well of you, lift you up when you are down, and enthusiastically applaud your successes. If our heart's desire is to embrace the noble mission of being a true Hero for others, if our concern for others is equal to our concern for ourselves, if we want to find favor with others, then remembering their name is but the first step in our journey to a greater and larger work. This larger work is realized when we commit ourselves to our work on a deeper and more meaningful level. The next chapter will show you how you can effectively acquire the proper Point of Focus.

3

DOING BUSINESS THE RIGHT WAY

J ust as I earlier encouraged you to write down and give the Covenant For Personal Relationships to others. So too, you should do the same in your business relationships. But, why a Covenant for business relationships? Because, when we pledge ourselves to upholding the terms of a covenant, we are in fact basing our business relationships on a very firm foundation of trust. Without the firm bedrock of trust as the foundation, then those that build upon it labor in vain.

Signing a covenant is serious business because you are committing yourself to the terms of the covenant. While it may be a serious matter, it need not be one that causes you to fear making such a commitment. Because when you've decided to live your life as a Hero for others, your signed covenant will be merely an outward expression of that which you highly value anyway.

A COVENANT FOR BUSINESS RELATIONSHIPS

Believing that my success depends on creating loyal customers both internal and external, I solemnly covenant these 10 principles to all persons with whom it is my privilege to serve.

1) I covenant to demonstrate integrity in all that I do. Each action I make, or word that I speak, will be done with complete honesty.

2) I covenant to be loyal to my company. I will defend the name of my company by doing everything within my power to make this a great place to work.

3) I covenant to respect the diversity in my place of work. Even though others are different from me, I will treat all others with the dignity and respect with which I too want to be treated.

4) I covenant to prepare myself for the future. I will use personal initiative to obtain the training that will be needed to face the competitive future with boldness.

5   I covenant to take personal responsibility for my actions and words. I will accept my portion of the blame when things go wrong and will not blame others for my errors.

6)   I covenant to speak well of my coworkers. I will always speak words of encouragement that will build up the morale of my workplace.

7)   I covenant to be trustworthy. I will not believe a partial story or repeat anything said to me in confidence.

8)   I covenant to maintain unity in my place of work. I will be the initiator to restore the spirit of unity among my coworkers.

9)   I covenant to be dedicated to quality. The quality of my work is but a reflection of my personal values and therefore it deserves my highest effort.

10)   I covenant to be a Hero for my customers. All of my actions and words will make my internal and external customers better off for having encountered me.

By: _____

Date: _____

To help you abide by the terms of this covenant, consider establishing a "Personal Board of Directors." Choose men and women that you respect from various disciplines and allow them to exercise influence in your life choices. (For example: Medicine, Law, Accounting, Clergy, Sales, Business Management, Marketing, etc.) Allow them to pour their knowledge into you, and agree to be held accountable to them regarding their area of expertise. Give each of them a signed copy of this covenant, and have regular meetings with each of them to assess your progress. Just as iron sharpens iron, so do wise people sharpen each other.

Abiding by the terms of this covenant will give your work a fresh and meaningful purpose. And, who knows, you just might get that raise you've been hoping for!

Section Six Summary

In business the stuff that matters most is developing loyal customers that are delighted to do business with you.

Know Why You Get Up in the Morning

Customer Service is the only good reason for going to work. In fact, it's the only reason you have a job! Answer this question: Is Customer Service _in_ you? Customer Service is not limited to a job description...it's a way of life.

DIMTY

"Do I Matter To YOU?" is the unspoken question that each of your customers (both internal and external) want you to answer for them.

Your Customer has a Name – Use it!

Differentiate yourself from your competitors by disciplining yourself to remember the names of all your customers. It's not hard to do, but it does require that you focus on what really matters – your customers! Remember, there is no sound sweeter to the ear of your customers than the sound of their own name.

A Covenant for Business Relationships

Establish a "Personal Board of Directors" consisting of people that you respect in disciplines that are not your area of expertise, and agree to be held accountable to them. To "raise the bar" and experience a workplace environment that is a joy to work in, let it be *you* that commits first to these covenants. Having the courage to do so will cause others to see your example and inspire them to do the same!

MISSION: IMPOSSIBLE?

♦ ♦ ♦

"Mr. Phelps," your assignment (should you decide to accept it) is to discover your mission in life by *applying* the principles contained in this section.

I loved watching the old "MISSION: IMPOSSIBLE" series on TV. Every week the characters were faced with seemingly impossible scenarios and obstacles to overcome. And, each week they succeeded. Their success was due in large part because they clearly understood what their mission was. Since they knew what their objective was, it was easy for them to take inventory of their abilities and they could clearly gauge their progress. Their mission for the week was delivered via an audio tape that would soon self-destruct. Therefore, knowing that the message would not be repeated, they had to listen carefully the first time to their instructions. These TV characters have a real advantage over us, because they knew beyond doubt precisely what their mission was. Unlike these characters which were given clear directives, each of us must make a personal choice regarding our mission in life.

Unfortunately, most people don't have much of a clue as to why they are here. They may be able to quote their company's mission statement at work, but not even have a personal mission statement as a guide for their life. Many of them wander through life never realizing that their life was designed to achieve a great and noble mission.

Of course, this whole subject of Personal Mission is deeply personal. In order to find your own personal mission, I invite you to look deep inside yourself and ask some very personal, probing, and revealing questions. Such as: Why were you born? What one word best describes your character? What do you value the most? What would those closest to you say that you value the most? What will be your legacy? Tough questions, huh? Well, I believe that questions often tell us more than answers ever do.

1

How *Old* are You?

P lease reread the question. The question is not, "What's your age?" It's "How *old* are you?" Most people respond to this question with a number. They think I want to know their age. But, regardless of your age, that is not necessarily how "old" you are. Think about it. How old you are doesn't depend upon your age. How old you are depends upon when you are going to die. For example: Let's say you're 30 years of age. Now, if you're going to live to age 90...you're young. But hey, if you're only going to make it to 35...you're "*old!*"

The Dash

I read of a man who stood to speak
at the funeral of his friend.
He referred to the dates on her tombstone
from the beginning...to the end.

He noted that first came the date of her birth
and spoke of the second with tears,
but he said that what mattered most of all
was the dash between those years.

For that dash represents all the time
that she spent alive on earth,
and now only those who loved her
know what that little line is worth.

For it matters not, how much we own;
the cars, the house, the cash.
What matters is how we live and love
and how we spend our dash.

So think about this long and hard,
are there things you'd like to change?
For you never know how much time is left.
You could be at dash "mid-range."

If we could just slow down enough to consider
what's true and what's real,
and always try to understand
the way other people feel.

And...be less quick to anger,
showing appreciation more
and love the people in our lives
like we've never loved before.

If we treat each other with respect,
and more often wear a smile,
remembering that this special dash
will only last a little while.

So, when your eulogy is being read
with your life's actions to rehash...
would you be pleased with the things
they have to say
about how you have spent your dash?

– Unknown

Of course this brings up the subject of death. And, since I fly over 100,000 miles per year, I'm often asked if I fear that the plane will crash. I guess I'm pretty fatalistic about it, because I usually say, "Well, if it's my time to go...it's my time to go." But, I got to thinking about this and asked myself, "Yeah, but what if it's the pilot's time to go?!"...I have to play his odds too! The problem is that none of us know how *old* we are...neither do the people in your family, your customers, or your friends. So, what's the point? The point is, since none of us know for certain how *old* we are, then now is the time to develop our Personal Mission statement.

2

WRITING YOUR PERSONAL MISSION STATEMENT

Imagine that you are riding in an elevator with your family. When the elevator stops, you will get off and never see them again. During this short amount of time, what would you say to your family? Obviously you would want to say "I love you." But, beyond that, what life principle would you encourage them to embrace?

I've found that this kind of "elevator-speak" is helpful in getting me focused on the core of what I truly want to say. Because the time is limited, I must phrase my statements in a brief and concise way. If too much time is allowed, I tend to ramble.

One day, while riding on an elevator, I challenged myself to come up with my Personal Mission Statement before the elevator stopped. Here it is: The day I was born, I cried, and the world rejoiced. I simply want to live my life in such a way, that on the day that I die the world cries, yet I rejoice!

You will notice that my personal mission statement is very broad in its scope, yet brief and concise. To fulfill this mission, it will require that all of my words and actions be in concert with its essence and meaning. At no time am I ever performing an action or speaking a word that is not under the umbrella of my personal mission statement. Because my personal mission statement is actually written, as opposed to merely a thought, I am consciously and subconsciously motivated to achieve it. It is imperative that it be written!

To write one for yourself, write down your answers to these questions:

1) What do you value the most? _____

_____

2) What is the current weekly cost (time & money) of that which you value the most?

Time _____ Money _____

3) What would those closest to you say that you value the most? (You may have to ask them.)

_____

4) Why were you born? _____

_____

5) What were you *designed* to become? _____

_____

6) What one word best describes you? _____

_____

7) What will be your one word legacy? _____

_____

8) What do you do in private when no one else is around you? _____

9) What are you naturally good at doing? _____

_____

10) Describe what your life will look like 5, 10, 20 years from now. _____

_____

11) What do you want? _____

_____

12) What activities bring you the greatest joy?

_____

13) Are your best days behind you, or are they ahead of you? _____

Are you starting to see a common thread running through each of your answers? If so, then write a sentence or two that will "raise the bar" for your behavior. Don't be timid, or think that you will never be able to achieve your mission. Remember, you are a human becoming...God's grandest creation! Because of this, you will find that by writing down your personal mission statement you will begin to consciously, and subconsciously, employ those behaviors that reflect the nobility of your personal mission statement. You will actually begin to make wise choices that are in step with your true values. You will heartily embrace each opportunity to make and honor commitments that drive you toward your purpose.

Write your personal mission statement here:

_____

_____

3

FULFILLING YOUR MISSION

Now that you have written your personal mission statement. Let's take a look at how you can make it become a reality every day. In order for each of us to live our lives on purpose, it is vital that we have the proper balance in our lives.

A properly "balanced" life is one that is equal and increasing in 4 areas: Mentally, Physically, Spiritually, and Socially. The perfect model of a properly balanced life can be found in Luke 2:52, "And Jesus increased in Wisdom, Stature, in favor with God, and in favor with Man." Jesus increased in Wisdom (Mentally), Stature (Physically, and in leadership ability), in favor with God (Spiritually), in favor with Man (Socially).

To help you picture what a perfectly balanced life looks like, visualize the following: Before you is a table with four legs. Each leg represents one of the four areas needed for proper balance; i.e. Mental, Physical, Spiritual, and Social. Upon the table rests a bowl of fruit. The bowl contains the fruit of the Spirit which is: "Love, Joy, Peace, Patience, Kindness, Goodness, Faithfulness, Gentleness, and Self-Control" - Gal 5:22. The bowl full of fruit remains on the table because the table is balanced. It's in a state of equilibrium. However, shortening or lengthening the legs at differing rates will result in an unbalanced table. And, anything placed upon such an unbalanced table is subject to sliding off of it.

One way to gauge whether or not your life is properly balanced is to look inside your bowl. Do you have all the fruit of the Spirit that is supposed to be in your bowl? If not, perhaps some of it fell out because the table wasn't properly balanced. The good news is that if you want your bowl to be full of the fruit of the Spirit, you can have it! All you have to do is make sure that the four legs of the table are all the same length. To do this let's take a closer look at those legs. The first is Wisdom.

4

INCREASING IN WISDOM

Wisdom is the ability to discern the best course of action in a given situation and then follow through and do it. Intelligence and wisdom are not one and the same. Intelligence has to do with what you know; while wisdom is the *proper application* of what you know. Each of us has, at one time or another, known what to do, but didn't do it. Our failure to do the right thing is most often not because of a lack of knowledge, but rather, a lack of willingness, or moral courage, to do what is right.

The scriptures tell us, "If anyone lacks wisdom, then let him ask of God. For God is the giver of all wisdom." - James 1:5. God does not desire for us to be fools. His desire is to see us operate in wisdom.

Four types of people:

He who knows not, and knows that he knows not is simple...teach him.

He who knows not, and knows not that he knows not is a fool...shun him.

He who knows, and knows not that he knows is asleep...waken him.

But, he who knows, and knows that he knows is wise...follow him!

– Unknown

We need to come to the point where we know, that we know, that we know. Knowing Him is the way to do this. Do you *know* God? Before you answer, consider this: Knowing God does not equal having heard about...read about...or even having met Him. For example: If I say that I know the President of the United States, maybe what I mean is that I know who he is. All of us know who he is because we have seen him on TV. However, very few people have actually met the President. These are the ones that have met him personally. Far fewer still are those that *know* him. For these are the people that share intimacy with the President. They have spent a lot of time with him and are likely to know how he thinks, how he reacts, what pleases him most, what makes him angry, how he feels, what his character is like...in short, they truly *know* him. To truly know anyone, including God, requires *intimacy* with the other person.

Recently, while playing golf with my pastor, I heard him laugh for the very first time (at a poor shot I'd made, obviously!) I was surprised to hear that his laugh sounded just like that of former NFL quarterback, Terry Bradshaw. Then it dawned on me that although I'd heard him preach many sermons, I'd never heard him laugh. Here was a man that I thought I knew, yet how could I presume to *know* him (or anyone else for that matter) if I don't even know what he sounds like when he laughs?

Then, I wondered, do I *know* God? If so, then what does His laugh sound like? I've been fortunate to have heard it many times: the unbridled joy that can best be expressed by a child's pure heart...the way that he allows me to goof-up (daily) and still see the humor in such a situation. I've seen His smile too: in the glory of spring flowers yawning as they awaken from a long winter's nap...in sunsets that seem to say, "Yeah, this was a beautiful day. 'Wonder if anyone noticed?" I've also tasted His tears of compassion. When I've been discouraged and worried about the future, His compassion has poured out to me in these words, "Do not worry about tomorrow. You cannot add a single hour to your life by worrying. I feed the birds of the air and clothe the flowers of the ground; how much more valuable are you than they?" - Matt. 6:25-34.

God desires to be intimate with you and me. He knows first hand how tough this life can be, and He doesn't want us to go through it alone. We all encounter trials and difficulties in life...the question is, are we going to have God's wisdom when we go through the trials? We can, if we have sought to know Him intimately – by spending time with Him...getting to know how He thinks...how He reacts...what pleases Him most...what makes Him angry...how He feels...what His character is like. Jesus Christ came to be our example *and* our savior. Jesus provided the way for us to be intimate with God. Jesus said, "I am the way, the truth, and the life. No one comes to the Father but by me." - John 14:6. It's not enough to know that He exists, or to have merely met Him. We must encounter God on His terms, not our own! We can do this by reading the Bible, praying continuously, singing His praises, worshipping Him, fellowshipping with other believers, and become wise enough to *actually do* what His word says to do! Then, and only then, will we be wise.

INCREASING IN STATURE

For each of us to increase in stature requires that we take good care of our bodies. Proper rest, exercise, food and drink all increase our ability to remain strong. With all my traveling it is seemingly impossible to eat right and exercise regularly. But, knowing the importance of keeping this leg of the table strong, I found a way.

First, I try to eat only good foods from the 4 main food groups: Cholesterol, Caffeine, Sodium, and French Fries! (Just kidding!) I do eat a careful balance of healthy food so that I will have the energy that I need each day. Since I fly, and have to eat at odd times, I take along a bag filled with carrots, sprouts, and broccoli for snacking. That way I'm not tempted to eat some high calorie food that will drag down my energy level.

Secondly, I find that I can exercise almost anywhere. Architects have built exercise equipment into virtually every building, (how thoughtful of them!). They are called stairs. All I do is check my bags at the Bell Desk and climb the stairs to my room. Once in the room I do pushups and stomach crunches. I do between 1,500-2,000 pushups every other day. These are done in sets of 100 - 200 repetitions spaced throughout the day. Since I can do 100 pushups in about one minute, my total workout time is 15-20 minutes. I do the stomach crunches anytime I'm watching TV or a video. Try this! You'll be surprised how many you can do during a viewing of the evening news.

Leadership

To increase in stature means not only physical growth but leadership ability as well. Leaders are defined by their followers. You see, if someone says that they're a "leader," but there's no one following them...they're just going for a walk!

When I speak at conferences to leaders of this nation's largest corporations and associations, I attend the concurrent and general sessions that precede mine. At these gatherings I listen to the other speakers and the attendees as they discuss the latest management trends. It's common to hear people quote from the most popular management books. They talk about the newest "management theorems"..."paradigm shifts"..."unarticulated directions"..."strategic thinking"...and other seemingly smart sounding, yet mind and heart-numbing, platitudes. But these leaders fail to realize that people don't follow "management theorems," "paradigm shifts," or any of the other lofty-sounding platitudes. They follow courage.

It takes courage to be an effective leader...one that gains a constituency of loyal followers by courageously leading through example, not platitudes. If you want to be an effective leader, then focus your life on behaving courageously...encouraging (giving courage to) your followers. History proves that people follow such courage.

Think of the greatest leaders from human history. Were they smarter than their followers?... probably not. Did they have more information?... probably not. Were they much stronger physically? ...probably not. Were they much better looking?... probably not. So, if they weren't smarter, more well informed, stronger, or better looking than their followers, then how come they were great leaders? The answer is...they had courage. The courage to believe in their principles...their ideals...to hold firm to their convictions regardless of how "unpopular" those ideals were at that time. They were uncompromising. Uncompromising men and women are easy to admire. They have the moral courage to fulfill their personal mission even to the point of death. Such conviction and courage is rare...that's why men follow after it.

When we say that someone is a person of great stature, we mean that they are highly esteemed by their peers. At an early age, Jesus was viewed by his peers as a leader. His sometimes odd behavior perplexed even his parents. One day he was separated from his parents, and his mother, Mary, wanted to know why he had stayed in the temple instead of traveling with the family. His response was, "Why were you worried about me? Did you not know that I would be in my Father's house?" - Luke 2:49. Even at an early age, Jesus made it clear that his life would be devoted to his personal mission. On this, he never compromised. He was willing to face persecution, slander, and ultimately death in pursuit of his mission.

Are we as passionate about our mission? Are we willing to run this race to its conclusion...the "Finish Line?" Life is not a sprint...it's a marathon. What would it take for us to stop running? A true leader, one of great stature, knows that the prize goes not to those who start the race, but to those who finish.

6

FINDING FAVOR WITH GOD

J esus found favor with God due to his intimate relationship with God. He diligently, and consistently, *applied* the scriptures to his life. To Him, the scriptures were not just the philosophical musings of some old dead dudes. They were the very foundation upon which He built His life. His obedience to <u>all</u> the scriptures sets Him apart from all the rest of us. Jesus, like no other, *actually did* all that the scriptures commanded Him to do. No wonder the Father spoke these words at his baptism, "This is My beloved son, in whom I am well-pleased." - Matt. 3:17.

Another person that found favor with God was Abraham. He was willing to sacrifice his only son Isaac, (a foreshadowing of the work God would do through His only son Jesus), simply because he was commanded by God to do it. Being a father myself, I don't know if I have the faith that Abraham demonstrated. If I were asked to do the same, I fear that my love for my son, Landon, might outweigh my devotion to God. Hopefully I'll never be tested in this way. But, because of Abraham's faithfulness it was considered as "his righteousness" by God - James 2:23. Therefore, we can safely conclude that nothing endears us to the heart of God like faith.

Our faith in God is most evident during times of trouble, trial, and tribulation. It is in these times that we must exercise our power to choose Him instead of choosing to worry. Here is a way that we can demonstrate our faithfulness to God...stop worrying. Worry happens when we place the burden of tomorrow on our shoulders today.

You know how it goes. You wake up in the morning with a sense of dread...caught up in a whirlpool of despair with seemingly no way out. All of your striving only weakens you as the current of catastrophe is pulling you under. Your mind is filled with thoughts of the failures of the past and anxiety for the future. You feel helpless in the present moment to do anything to stop these fears. That, my friend, is an illusion. The reality is that you *can* stop worrying!

When I am stressed and feel an almost overpowering presence of hopelessness and despair, that's when I turn my eyes upon Him. This is done by, "taking every thought captive." - 2 Cor. 10:5. That is, when I am tempted by negative feelings and a fear of failure, I choose to compare my fears to the faithfulness of my God. In these times, I think and actually say the following out loud:

> What are my failures compared to His faithfulness?

> What are my fears compared to His fierce love for me?

> What is my striving compared to His salvation?

> What are my many cares compared to His compassion?

> What are my problems compared to the promises He has for me?

By taking the negative thoughts captive in this way, I am exercising my power of choice. And guess what?...the fears, depression, and anxiety stop and are replaced by a spirit of peace. And then I experience "the peace that passes all comprehension,"– His peace. You see, if it's a peace that you can comprehend, it may not be His peace. For example: If your peace is born from the womb of plenty – an abundance of good health, prosperity, and strong relationships – then maybe the source of your peace is entirely *comprehensible.*

On the other hand, if you are experiencing peace without having an abundance of good health, prosperity, and strong relationships, you are probably experiencing the peace that God promises to us by His Spirit..."I give to you a peace that passes all *comprehension*." - Phil 4:6,7.

As a businessman and father, I've learned to trust in Him. By doing so, I've discovered:

His faithfulness never fails!

His fierce love for me casts away all fear!

His salvation surpasses all of my striving!

His compassion conquers my many cares!

His promises provide a way out of any problem that I'm facing!

What loving father can refuse the cry of his child? So too, if we cry out to God, He will surely wipe away our tears. This, my friend, gives me great hope...a hope not based on my own intellect, financial resources, good health, or human relationships – because any or all of these are subject to change – but rather a hope that is based on the unchanging character of my Creator.

7

FINDING FAVOR WITH MAN

J esus found favor with man chiefly through influence. He was able to influence his generation, and indeed ours as well, through the content of his character. To his friends and enemies alike, he was viewed as a person standing firmly on an unshakable foundation.

So, it is true even today. We all admire people of strong character...people who build their lives upon a firm foundation. However, instead of focusing on people, let's take a look at the foundation. We will focus on the foundation because, if properly built, it will stand the test of time.

The blueprint for a firm foundation can be found in Matthew 7:24-29 and in Luke 6:46-49. There you will find a comparison between two types of people...one who is wise...and one that is a fool.

The fool is the one that having decided to build a house, does so upon a foundation of shifting sand. Over time the rains fall, the flood waters rise, and the wind blows against it. Naturally, a house built upon such a weak and shifting foundation will surely collapse. In time it will be seen that foolish is the man that, having heard God's word, refuses to obey. The more we hear of God's word and the less we change...the harder our heart will become.

The wise person is the one that dug deep, removing the dirt, and laid his foundation upon the rock. When the flood rose and the torrent burst against the house, it could not be shaken.

To properly understand the symbolism in this illustration, I offer the following glossary of terms: Dirt = anything other than Christ, Rock = Christ, House = a life, Torrent = the trials of life, Foundation = Faith.

Now, if you reread the story, substituting in the definitions above, you will see the true meaning of this scripture. Luke 6:47,48,49 – **47** "Everyone who comes to Me, and hears My words, and acts upon them, I will show you whom he is like: **48** he is like a man building a house (a life), who dug deep (removing the dirt...anything other than Christ), and laid a foundation (faith) upon the rock (Christ); and when the flood rose, the torrent (the trials of life) burst against that house (a life) and could not shake it, because it had been well built. **49** But, the one who has heard, and has not *acted accordingly*, is like a man who built his house (a life) upon the dirt (anything other than Christ) without any foundation (faith); and the torrent (the trials of life) burst against it and immediately it collapsed, and the ruin of that house (a life) was great."

If we are to be wise we will not be content to merely hear His words...we will act upon them. If we are to be strong in character, if we are to endure the trials of life, then we must place our full faith in Christ alone. Only a foundation built upon His unchangeable character is capable of protecting those that reside in the house.

So, the message and meaning for each of us is clear. We can build a life that reflects the character of God when we choose to establish as the foundation for our lives the unchangeable character of God.

If you are wise enough to build such a foundation others will notice how you weather the storms of life. They will see that you, unlike many of them, have not been shaken by adversity or buckled under the winds of change. They will see your strength, your resolve, your relaxed mental attitude in the midst of turmoil, and desire the same results that your wise choices have produced. You will be providing for them a living blueprint for success in life. You will have found favor with them.

So, "Mr. Phelps," what's your decision? Are you going to accept your mission? I hope you can see that with God's help it *really is* <u>not</u> impossible!

SECTION SEVEN SUMMARY

How Old Are You?

We can't truly know how "*old*" we are, so <u>now</u> is the time to develop our Personal Mission statement.

Writing Your Personal Mission Statement

Please actually write in your answers. Putting it in writing will make you both consciously and subconsciously aware of your mission.

Fulfilling Your Mission

This requires a balanced life in four areas: Wisdom (mentally), Stature (physically, and leadership ability as well), In Favor with God (spiritually), and In Favor with Man (socially).

Increasing in Wisdom

Intelligence does not equal wisdom. Intelligence is what you know, and wisdom is the *proper application* of what you know. We can become wise by developing an *intimate* relationship with God.

Increasing in Stature

"Stature" implies physical growth as well as leadership ability. Physical growth: a proper balance of rest, exercise, food, and drink are essential for healthy physical growth. Even with a hectic schedule it is possible to make this a priority. Leadership ability: history proves that effective leaders behave courageously...encouraging (giving courage to) their followers.

In Favor with God

An active and obvious faith is what pleases God. When we find favor with God, we experience a peace that passes all comprehension.

In Favor with Man

Develop in you the unchangeable character of God by first establishing a rock-solid foundation for your life. Others will see your strength in times of trial and be drawn to you.

RESILIENCY

♦ ♦ ♦

Resiliency is the ability to snap back after being stretched. Take a rubber band and stretch it until it almost breaks and then let go. It will snap back to its original size and will also release a great deal of energy when it does. The same is true with a balloon. It can be blown-up to almost the breaking point, but if the air escapes, it will return to its original condition.

This final section deals with people that have been stretched to the very point of breaking, yet have snapped back to live successful lives.

1

A MASTERFUL DESIGN

There is a common trait shared among most people that are truly resilient...they handle their hurts in a very productive way. Resilient people are those that are wise enough to trust in a Higher Power instead of shouldering all the burden of life's many cares alone.

Have you ever had a problem with a product that you bought at a store? Perhaps it was that blender that just doesn't seem to know the difference between "mix" and "puree." Or, the hair dryer that no longer dries your hair...the electric toothbrush that no longer vibrates...the computer that "can't find printer." (Once this happened to me and I simply turned my monitor to face the printer and told it, "There it is!") We all know how frustrating it can be when something that we depend on no longer works properly. Most folks, when faced with a broken gadget will either try to repair it themselves...or take it back to the manufacturer.

Taking a broken product back to the manufacturer for repairs makes good sense, because the manufacturer designed it and knows how it is supposed to function. The manufacturer designed the blueprint, assembled the parts, and is best suited to perform any needed repairs.

We too were designed by our "manufacturer" to function properly. Why then do we, when things fall apart, not take our problem back to our manufacturer. All too often we try to "fix" the problems of our lives by ourselves. By doing so, we waste far too much time and energy, and usually end up screwing up our lives even more! Only then do we throw up our hands in desperation and ask our manufacturer to help us. It doesn't have to be this way, because each of us has an Owner's Manual available to us. It's called The Bible. But, like most Owner's Manuals, it is rarely read. What's that saying? "When all else fails...read the directions!"

Let us then look to our "manufacturer" for help in the proper function of our lives. He designed us to achieve and wants our lives to function properly. Indeed, He is committed to excellence in customer service! He wants what is best for us, even more than we do! He is available 24 hours a day to help us, and he backs his creation with a "Lifetime Warranty!" Anytime we have a problem, all we have to do is trust Him with it. And, He will never ask to see a receipt! (Thank God!)

2

APRIL 19, 1995

On April 19, 1995, something tragic happened that changed our world forever. On that day, a madman ignited a bomb outside the Alfred P. Murrah Building in Oklahoma City. The result of the explosion was the loss of 168 lives, hundreds more injured, and families, indeed a nation, stretched to the breaking point.

We will never forget the media images from that day that are burned into our collective consciousness. It was a wake-up call for America...that hate and terrorism are not limited to the boundaries of the Middle East, but that hate and evil are alive and well even in the heartland of America.

One year after the bombing, I was hired to speak to the survivors and their families. The Salvation Army, which was highly instrumental in providing much needed logistical and physical help on the day of the bombing and the months that followed, was hosting an event for the survivors and family members of the bombing victims. Instead of holding the event on the first anniversary of the bombing, they chose to have it one week later, April 26, 1996. The Salvation Army provided buses to take these good people to their encampment outside of Tulsa, Oklahoma.

The purpose of this event was to allow these people to have some fun, away from the pressure of the press, and to minister to them. Approximately 400 of them arrived on Friday to begin a weekend of renewal.

For over a year these people had been stretched to the breaking point. Many of them were tired, weary, frustrated, confused, and in need of refreshment. The Salvation Army did a masterful job of orchestrating an entire weekend that was designed to help them relax, play, and simply enjoy some time with each other. They put up inflatable games like bungee football; had fishing, hayrides, many activities for the kids; they even had Sumo wrestling! Most of all, the Salvation Army provided a relaxed atmosphere for God to minister to them with his peace.

It was in this setting that I was to speak. What an awesome privilege and responsibility it was.

I've been hired for tough assignments before, but never one that approached the emotional struggle of this one. How could I possibly have anything to say to a group of people that had been through what they had? Naturally, I felt totally inadequate for the job. Therefore, I enlisted the help of many others. I wrote a "Prayer Summons" and sent it to many of my friends and fellow speakers asking them to pray for me and the people in attendance. At the time, I received many calls and letters from friends and speakers like Zig Ziglar, Og Mandino, and Naomi Rhode. Knowing that many others were praying about this really helped to put me at ease as I faced the most important speaking engagement of my life.

My message to them was that they have a future...a future that is brimming with hope and promise. Although they have experienced a loss of unimaginable magnitude, the Holy Spirit of God is available to lovingly comfort them. My Keynote contained a great deal of entertainment and humor as well as a message of hope and renewal. It was a joy to look at their smiling faces...many faces that had not laughed in over a year.

Perhaps the most touching moment of all was when a young African American woman that had lost her husband in the bombing came up and took my hand, looked into my eyes, and simply told me, "I love you." I knew from her response, and the response of hundreds more, that the message of renewal had reached their souls. I saw parents that had lost their child, yet had started to have more children. There were grandparents, now forced to raise their grandchildren, that could simply relax for a few days while someone else took care of the little ones.

Yes, their lives had been stretched like a rubber band to its breaking point, but during that weekend much of the tension was eased. And, the families and survivors of this great tragedy revealed through their courage, smiles, and laughter how very resilient they truly are.

3

ILLUSION VS. REALITY

As an illusionist, it is my job to suspend the moment of disbelief that the audience members have so they will wonder, "Did what I just see *really* happen?!" And, while I may enjoy fooling my audiences from the stage, my purpose in writing this book is so that you would *not* be deceived.

Our perception of ourselves, and of our purpose, will dictate how resilient we are during the inevitable trials of life. Because, the more centered we are in our purpose, the easier it is to make wise choices and honor our commitments while under fire. The following questions will help you determine which of these two belief systems you most readily embrace. And, the following comparison of these two beliefs systems will reveal what you believe to be an illusion and what you believe to be reality.

But, first, the questions. Your answers to these questions will provide clues regarding your belief system.

Are you just taking up space?

Do you believe that you were created to fulfill some great and noble purpose?

Were you designed to stand apart from the crowd?

Are you haunted by memories of your past failures?

Are you loved unconditionally?

Is your value as a person tied to performance on the job and in the home?

Do you believe in scarcity or abundance?

Does your life lack purposeful direction?

Have you "arrived?"

Are your best days behind you?

What one word would most accurately describe you?

What word would you put in this blank? – "I am _____ ."

I would fill-in that blank with "wonderful!" because I was raised to believe that I am wonderful. My parents did not foster this belief in me based on what I did or on some task that I performed, but rather "I am wonderful!" simply because God created me to be that way. But, before you write me off as an egotist, please let me explain.

Many people would not characterize themselves as "wonderful!", but would say something like, "I am just a sinner saved by grace." And while it's true that all of us have sinned, we are not defined according to scripture by our actions alone, but by His grace. We have been saved *by* grace, but <u>*because*</u> of love. - John 3:16. Love is the motivation, and grace is the by-product. We are not "sinners"...we are the beloved of God! Any word that follows the words "I am ____" needs to be carefully considered in light of how *God* describes us. I can say with confidence that "I am wonderful!" because His word says that I am, "fearfully and wonderfully made!" - Ps. 139:14. Therefore, all that I do flows out of that belief.

This belief has given me great confidence that I can accomplish anything. Although I'm not always successful at everything that I do, I still believe that the future is going to be favorable...that my best days are yet to come. Some folks would call that "denial!" But, I don't think so. God gave me breath this morning for some reason...to finish something...to improve...to become...

Further, this belief has carried me through many an hour of depression...thoughts that have haunted my mind with imaginings of impending doom, disaster, and despair. Whenever these thoughts enter my mind, I quickly cut them off before they can take root in my spirit. I do this by ceasing to dwell on these things and returning to the belief that my God has a bright and wonderfully blessed future in store for me. Because I am His child, then I am an heir to all that He has. And, He has everything! So, why would I worry about my apparent lack in light of all that He has and that He freely wants to give me?! We live our lives with either the belief in scarcity or the belief in abundance. I choose to believe in abundance, because Jesus himself promised, "I have come that you might have life, and have it more abundantly!" - John 10:10. Therefore, when I am tempted to focus on the apparent lack of my resources, I look to God to make up the difference in what I lack. And, guess what? He has never failed me!

Now, let's look at two opposing belief systems. One is an illusion, while the other is reality.

<u>**Illusionary Belief**</u>	<u>**Reality Based Belief**</u>
"I can't..."	"I can do *all things* throughChrist who strengthens me!" - Phil. 4:13
"I am just an accident"	"I *was chosen* in Christ before the foundation of the world to be holy and without blame before Him." - Eph. 1:4
"I am poor."	"I am an *heir* of God since I am a son of God." - Gal. 4:6,7
"I am not worthy of love."	"God has bestowed a great love on me and called me his *child.*" - 1 John 3:1
"I am not smart."	"I have been given the mind of Christ." - 1 Cor. 2:16
"My future looks uncertain."	"For I *know* the plans I have for *you*...to give you a future and a hope." - Jer. 29:11-13
"My life lacks direction."	"Trust in the Lord with all your heart, lean not on your own understanding, in all your ways acknowledge Him, and He will *direct* your paths." - Prov. 3:5,6

"I am 'yesterday's news.'"	"Therefore if any man is in Christ, he is a *new creature*; the old things are passed away; behold, all things have become new." - 2 Cor. 5:17
"I don't have a friend."	"I am Christ's *friend*." - John 15:13-15
"Even God is ashamed of me."	"Because I am sanctified and am one with Christ, He is not ashamed to call me His." - Heb. 2:11
"I'm no different than everyone else."	"I have been saved and *set apart* according to God's purpose and grace." - 2 Tim. 1:9
"I am not significant."	"I am part of a chosen race, a royal priesthood, a holy nation, a people of God's own possession." - 1 Peter 2:9,10
"I am a coward."	"For God has not given us a spirit of timidity, but of *power*, and love, and discipline."- 2 Tim. 1:7
"I am weak."	"The Lord is my *strength* and my shield; My heart trusts in Him, and I am helped." - Ps. 28:7

"I can't talk to God."	"I may come *boldly* before the throne of God to receive mercy and find grace to help me in time of need." - Heb. 4:16
"I don't have a father."	"I am a *son* of God." (God is literally my "Papa.") - Gal. 4:6
"I am unloved."	"For I am *convinced* that neither death nor life, neither angels nor demons, neither the present nor the future nor any powers, neither height nor depth, nor *anything* in all creation, will be able to separate us from the love of God that is in Christ Jesus our Lord." - Rom. 8:38,39
"I am not well-liked."	"The Lord *delights* in His people." - Ps. 149:4

Just one more question: Why does God get up in the morning?...to see you!...to experience the day with you. *You* are His reason for joy! This is not to say that the entire universe revolves around you...it doesn't. But, this day was given to you as an opportunity for you to live it in partnership with your God. You are the delight of His heart and He can't wait to see what the two of you will do today! He is like a loving father that enters his child's nursery early in the morning because he wants to be the first thing his child sees that day.

When my children were little, I would go into their room and stand peering over their cribs as I softly called them by name. As their tiny eyes slowly opened, the first thing they saw was my face. Then, they would lift their arms up as they smiled and said, "Papa, hold me."

Those moments are some of the most precious in my memory. Because of my delight in them, I would take them into my arms and carry them throughout the day. So it is with our heavenly father. He whispers our name each morning and longs for us to reach out and say, "Papa, hold me." The world can be a big and scary place, but somehow everything seems to be all right if our Papa is there to hold us in his arms of love.

4

MY ENCOUNTER
WITH TRUTH

Now, I would like to tell you a story about the person that has had the most profound influence on my life. I often refer to him as my "Hero."

When I was a Freshman in High School, our varsity football team was a very good one. We were 5-A State Semi-Finalists in Texas. The school was, and still is, the largest in the state of Texas. There was a boy on our team that was the Captain, a linebacker, a strong, good-looking young man. This boy was President of the Fellowship of Christian Athletes, a dedicated student, and a young man of strong moral character. However, he is not the hero in this story.

The hero is that boy's father, because his father did something highly unusual. He went to every game, and every practice for 4 years. Every *practice!* And, no, he was not the coach. He was a salesman that carved time out of his schedule every afternoon, to be on the sideline watching his son practice football. It was a real inspiration for all of us as we watched this father be there every day for his son.

You might be wondering if the sacrifice and commitment that this father made paid off. I think he would say that it did. Because, one day while his son was practicing football, that 17 year old son of his dropped dead...of a massive heart attack. As it turned out, this boy was 17 years "old." We were all stunned. The entire school couldn't believe that such a young man would die so suddenly in this way.

At the funeral, I watched carefully as the father passed by the casket, bent down, and kissed his son good-bye for the last time. I looked in his eyes when he came up, and expected to see tears. But, instead I saw a smile. A smile? Yes. Because here was a man that had no regrets. He didn't have to say, "If I'd just done a little bit more...If I just had a little more time...One more day, just give me *one more day* to show him that I love him!"

The boy was my brother...and the father is my dad.

After my older brother Wendy died, I was devastated. I'd lost my best friend, and I felt so very lonely. At that time, I sought to soothe my pain by filling my mind with the popular self-help books of the day. I'm sure that the authors of those books were well-meaning; however, their man-made philosophies were totally inadequate to comfort my tortured soul. You see, my heart had a God-shaped hole in it that only God could fill. In desperation, I cried out, "God help me!" and immediately He wrapped me in his arms of love while tenderly restoring my broken heart.

I learned a lot from that. I learned that the choices that we make and the commitments that we honor are ultimately all that *really* matter.

And, for you the reader of this book, my hope is that you will make wise choices and honor your commitments...that you would have the courage to become all that you were designed by God to become...that you would not resist this change, but become an ambassador *for* change...changing the lives of others...one person at a time...one encounter at a time.

If you will take personal responsibility for the messages this book contains, then my writing it has not been in vain and your future will be a most magical one indeed!

Section Eight Summary

A Masterful Design

When their life is broken, a resilient person will consult their Owners Manual and seek the wise counsel of their Manufacturer.

April 19, 1995

After the bombing of the Alfred P. Murrah building in Oklahoma City, many of the survivors demonstrated just how resilient they truly are.

Illusion vs. Reality

The belief system that we embrace will determine how resilient we will be during the storms of life.

My Encounter with Truth

After hitting the bottom of an emotional pit of despair, God heard my cry for help and healed my broken heart.

RECOMMENDED READING

Improving Your Parenting - John Offutt

Doin' Time - Rick Nielsen & Ron Kuntz

Will You Remember Uncle Sam in Your Will? - Dave Nielsen

The Hiding Place - Corrie Ten Boom

The Scarlet Pimpernel - Orczy

Joshua - Joseph F. Girzone

The Greatest Salesman In The World - Og Mandino

The Chronicles of Narnia - C.S. Lewis

The Screwtape Letters - C.S. Lewis

The Jesus I Never Knew - Philip Yancey

The Song of Albion Trilogy - Stephen Lawhead

The Dragon King Trilogy - Stephen Lawhead

Charlotte's Web - E.B. White

The Hobbit - J.R.R. Tolkien

The Lord of the Rings Trilogy - J.R.R. Tolkien

Anything Written by Max Lucado

Recommended Viewing

Braveheart

Sound of Music

Jesus of Nazareth

Star Wars Trilogy

8 Seconds

It's a Wonderful Life

City of Angels

Rocky

To Kill a Mockingbird

Field Of Dreams

The Ten Commandments

Babe

Spartacus

Harvey

Ben Hur

ABOUT THE AUTHOR

Andy is a Professional Speaker that combines good clean humor...amazing illusions...and a highly customized message that entertains, educates, motivates, challenges, and inspires his audiences.

Andy has earned the CSP (Certified Speaking Professional) designation from the National Speakers Association. The CSP is the highest earned designation awarded by NSA. Additionally, less than 10% of the professional speakers in NSA have earned the CSP designation.

It was while working with David Copperfield's "Project Magic" that Andy realized magic could be used as a tool to both entertain and inspire others. Since 1991, Andy has had the privilege of keynoting for some of the nation's largest corporations, associations, and many church/

non-profit organizations as well. He would love to have the opportunity to speak for your people too!

Andy's keynote topics include:

Motivational
"The magic of the Future is YOU!"

Managing Change
"The Bonsai Principle"

Customer Service
"Is Customer Service IN You?!"

Personal Development
"Stuff That Really Matters"

His memory workshop is titled, "How to make an Unforgettable Impression."

For further information on Andy's speaking services, products, or if ya' want to say "Hi!"... contact your favorite speakers bureau or:

Andy Hickman, CSP
PO Box 181569
Dallas TX 75218
800-947-0486
www.AndyHickman.com

Andy Hickman
PRODUCT ORDER FORM

Individual Title	Qty	Amount
Stuff That Really Matters — Book $11.95		
Stuff That Really Matters — Audio Book $19.95		
The Magic of the Future is YOU! — Audio Tape $10.95		

Please add $3 shipping & handling for 1 book
and $1 s/h for each additional book.

Sub Total

S/H

TOTAL

Andy Hickman
P.O. Box 181569 • Dallas TX 75218
Phone/Fax 800 947-0486
On the web at:
www.andyhickman.com
urmagic@aol.com

Name _____ Date _____

Company _____

Street Address _____

City/Province _____ State _____

Zip/Postal Code _____ Country _____ Day Phone _____

☐ **YES** — *Please send me information on Andy Hickman's speaking services.*

☐ VISA
☐ MC | Card
☐ DISC. | No. / / / / / / / / / / / / / / / / / /

Exp. date _____ Signature _____